GUERILLA WARFARE ON THE AMBER COAST

Guerilla Warfare on the Amber Coast

by

K. V. TAURAS

VOYAGES PRESS

I hold it a noble task to rescue from oblivion those who deserve to be eternally remembered.

—Pliny the Younger

TABLE OF CONTENTS

GUERILLA WARFARE ON
THE AMBER COAST

AUTHOR'S PREFACE

The historical narrative which unfolds in the following pages is almost completely unknown to Western readers. *Guerilla Warfare on the Amber Coast* is an authentic, factual history of Lithuanian resistance against Soviet and Nazi oppressors between 1940-1952. This report is based on first-person accounts supplied by people who lived in Lithuania and who were able to reach the West; on statements by defected Soviet officials and military personnel. on articles of the Lithuanian underground press; and on items which have appeared openly in official Communist releases. For the most part, the report concentrates on Lithuanian guerilla operations against the Soviet colonial administration in Lithuania between 1944 and 1952.

Most of the first-hand experiences in this narrative were brought to the West by Juozas Luksa, a special emissary from the Lithuanian Freedom Army to Lithuanian institutions in the free world. As a freedom fighter he had used the aliases of *Skrajunas, J. Daumantas,* and *Miškinis.* In 1950 he returned to Soviet-occupied Lithuania to rejoin the LFA. According to Soviet sources, the NKVD captured and executed him in about October, 1951.

This narrative is published for the record and in the belief that it may serve a useful purpose at this particular juncture in world affairs. Interested readers will find extensive documentation and first-hand accounts of guerilla operations of the Lithuanian Freedom Army in the publications listed at the end of this report.

K. V. TAURAS

New York City

xi

INTRODUCTION

Although most of us have never visited Lithuania, the "Amber Coast" of the title, we are by no means unfamiliar with the tragic tale of the small nation, imbued with traditions as deep as the roots of its people, taking up arms against a gigantic invader. Perhaps most real to us of all these events in recent times is the Hungarian Revolution of 1956 which was played out on the world's stage to a world-wide audience and became one of freedom's most historic acts of faith.

This was an experience indelibly engraved upon the entire free world. Of the struggle in Lithuania, we knew much less, and yet the memory of Hungary's few tragic days of freedom should help us in some measure to comprehend the sacrifice, the courage and the indomitable will of the Lithuanians whose story is told in the pages that follow.

In the past decade, too, we have become familiar with Soviet "wars of national liberation." We have seen Soviet tanks as they approached to *liberate* Budapest. We have seen Cuba and the Cuban people as they have been *liberated* by Fidel Castro. We have now in Europe and in our own country many refugees who have fled in ragged terror from the glories of Soviet *liberation*. There is reflected in the faces of these exiles, many of them Lithuanian, a frustration and tragic loss which dwarfs even the most generous compassion extended to them by those living freely in the West. This book tells of some of these people who, risking their lives and

1

everything else they had, determined that in Lithuania, at least, the spark of their nation would be kept alive.

It is not our business here to review the history of Lithuania. The history of this northern Baltic nation, now absorbed into the Union of Soviet Socialist Republics, is covered adequately enough for our purposes in the opening chapters of this book. Just as the Baltic Sea casts up pieces of amber on her shores when the wind whips the waves to fury, so, too, history throws upon this small nation the crises that ravage her hemisphere.

Since the Eleventh Century, Lithuania has been embroiled in the conflicts raging across Europe. In our own century alone she has been the victim of treachery which resulted in invasion by Germany from the west and usurpation by Russia from the east. Despite decades of cruel domination, however, the spirit of this nation has not broken. Quite the contrary, it has steadfastly persevered without even the spotlight of history to encourage it.

The story of the Lithuanian Freedom Army (LFA) fighting with inferior weapons but superior will against the brutal NKVD forces, daring to print and circulate newspapers and posters, destroying records of patriots, inciting the people to boycott mock elections, protecting the property of deported citizens, raiding Soviet supplies, rescuing many of those doomed to mass deportation—in short, people dedicated to the will to resist tyranny—has much to teach us in the West.

There is much in the so-called "peaceful" nation of Lithuania that parallels the so-called "peaceful" world today. In Lithuania from 1944 to 1952, no armies clashed on battlefields. No tanks engaged enemy tanks in battle. No war, as too many of us have come to define war, existed. And yet, neither was there peace—peace as we were once taught to expect it.

Small, highly organized, effective groups of guerillas thwarted within Lithuania the Soviet plans for collectivization. Small steel-nerved groups assassinated Soviet terrormasters sent to subdue their nation. Small unarmed groups of literate men wrote and distributed material denying the legality of Russian occupation and encouraging the people to resist. At no time were these groups who made up the Lithuanian Freedom Army of substantial size. At no time did they delude themselves into believing that they could drive the Soviets out of their nation. Their object was rather to harass, to delay, to attract the attention of the West, and above all to remind the people that they were victims of aggression, not partners in the "glorious Soviet state."

In a world where this book can be written, peace alone is not and cannot be the proper objective of effective diplomacy. Peace alone cannot be the objective in a world where slavery is foisted upon whole nations under the guise of "democracy"; where blatant imperialist aggression is camouflaged as a "war of national liberation." Hungary and Lithuania are but two of those already sacrificed to this kind of diplomacy.

There are episodes to come in this book which may shock and repel those who have come to regard modern warfare as either neatly uniformed armies facing each other across barricades or nuclear holocaust too horrible to envision. Guerilla warfare is brutality seen close up. But as our own government has belatedly come to realize, it is an effective weapon in many

3

of the small nations currently slated for Soviet *liberation*.

The LFA has much to teach us of guerilla tactics. A small band of highly mobile, supremely trained forces disciplined to silent, effective action, in the years from 1944 to 1952, succeeded in thwarting major Soviet objectives and kept alive in their country the sense of national unity which today distinguishes Lithuania from any other Soviet Republic. And all this done with no illusion of final victory!

Today, the LFA is disbanded, its members like shadows absorbed into the people once again. Farm collectivization, Soviet troop reinforcements ultimately forced these soldiers to concentrate on peaceful resistance, a resistance which is not without its effects today in Lithuania. Perhaps it is inherent in the democracies of the West that we recognize crisis belatedly. Perhaps it is also characteristic that we react, at least initially, in an inadequate manner. But it is not and cannot be inherent that free men fail totally to recognize the jeopardy they share.

Guerilla Warfare On The Amber Coast is, above all, a personal document. It transcends factional interests. It is a story of men dedicated to an ideal beyond themselves and committed to the defense of that ideal in any and all ways consistent with their heritage. As such, it should be ours as well as his who lived and wrote it.

We should not be deaf to the meaning that is here for us as we make our decisions on Cuba, on Laos, on Vietnam, on the Congo—for there is a warning here for us as well. From the freedom fighter who wrote this book, come these words: "As the periphery of the Free World is eroded by incessant Soviet and Communist Chinese manoeuvres, it

4

would be well to remember that the West does not possess an endless supply of small nations, the sacrifice of which, some may still unrealistically hope, will indefinitely postpone a confrontation between the Free World and a dehumanized totalitarianism . . ."

LEO CHERNE

New York
January 3, 1962

I.

LITHUANIA BEFORE WORLD WAR II

There is no such thing as a small country. . . . Whoever presents a great example is great.

—Victor Hugo

LITHUANIA THROUGH THE AGES

Lithuania is situated on the eastern shore of the Baltic Sea. To the north lies Latvia; to the east, Byelorussia; to the south, Poland; and to the west, the so-called Kaliningradskaya Oblast (prewar East Prussia) and the Baltic Sea.

On stormy days the waves of the Baltic Sea cast up pieces of amber on the beaches. For this reason the Baltic Coast from the Lithuanian resort town of Palanga to the Polish port of Gdansk is known to geographers as the "Amber Coast."

With her 25,213 square miles, Lithuania is somewhat larger than Switzerland, Belgium or Denmark. According to the Soviet census of January 15, 1959, she now has a population of 2,711,000. In 1939, however, the population in this same area was 3,215,000, and under normal conditions should have increased to 3,900,000 by 1959. These huge population losses are the result of Soviet and Nazi genocide.

The principal cities of Lithuania are: Vilnius (235,000), Kaunas (214,000), Klaipedas (89,000), and Shiauliai

6

(60,000). Farming remains the main occupation of her inhabitants, despite industrialization efforts made during the last decade. Roman Catholicism, the principal religion, claims 84.5 per cent of the population, according to prewar data.

Lithuania is not a "new state," either politically or culturally. She is as old as most European nations, and her history abounds in drama.

The Lithuanians of today are a survival of a separate and distinct branch of the Aryan family, and are not members of the Slavonic or Germanic lineage. Their language differs as completely from those neighboring tongues as, for instance, English differs from Greek. Professor Benjamin D. Dwight wrote: "Lithuanian is a language of great value to the philologist. It is the most antique in its forms of all the living languages of the world, and most akin in its substance and spirit to the primeval Sanskrit."

Lithuanians lived on the Baltic shores long before the Christian era, and at the dawn of European history had attained a level of civilization equal to that of many other European nations of those days. The Roman historian Tacitus, who lived in the first century A.D., mentions the Lithuanians as good cultivators of the soil. Eminent German scientists, such as Tischler and Bezzenberger, admired the excellent workmanship revealed in bronze articles found in early tombs of the ancient Lithuanians.

The recorded history of the independent Lithuanian State dates back to the eleventh century A.D. At the beginning of the thirteenth century the German Orders of the Sword-bearers and the Crusaders (later known as the Teutonic Knights) began a ruthless warfare against the Lithuanians.

The western area of the country, known as Lithuania Minor, suffered greatly from the onslaught of the German Orders, yet these did not succeed in their effort to conquer the entire country. In 1410, Lithuania, together with Poland, inflicted a crushing defeat on the Teutonic Knights at Zhalgiris (Tannenberg).

In the fifteenth century Lithuania's rapid expansion advanced her to the rank of a great East European Power. Her territories stretched from the Baltic to the Black Sea, embracing Byelorussia and the Ukraine. Then, in 1569, in Lublin, Lithuania and Poland concluded a treaty of confederation which established the Lithuanian-Polish Commonwealth.

From the sixteenth century on, the growing power of Muscowy became an increasing menace to Lithuania's territorial integrity and even to her independence. As Zygmunt-August, King of the Lithuanian-Polish Commonwealth, expressed in his letter to Queen Elisabeth I of England, dated July 13, 1567: "The more Moscow's power grows, the greater the danger not only to us but to all Christianity."*

Moscow's expansionism was not the only cause of the decline of the Lithuanian-Polish Commonwealth. The wars with Sweden and the internal strife weakened the Commonwealth to such a degree that in the eighteenth century it was divided between Russia, Prussia and Austria (1772-1795). The greater part of Lithuania was acquired by Russia.

The Russian domination of Lithuania continued from 1795 to 1915, when the German armies occupied the coun-

---

* Since the period of Czar Ivan III (1440-1505), Russia has fought 86 aggressive wars (12 under the Soviets), and perpetrated 89 annexations of territories, 20 of them by the Soviets.

try. Yet the Lithuanians never lost their hope to regain freedom and independence. The period of Russian rule shows a succession of revolts against the Muscovite oppressors: 1797, 1812, 1831, 1863, and 1905.

The brutality and inefficiency of the Russian regime retarded Lithuania's economic and cultural development. The country stagnated. Many Lithuanians emigrated to the New World and settled in the United States, Canada and some Latin-American countries.

INDEPENDENCE REGAINED

World War I provided the Lithuanians with a long-awaited opportunity. With the country still under German military occupation, a Lithuanian Council proclaimed the restoration of Lithuania's independence on February 16, 1918. An ill-equipped army, hastily organized after the armistice, held its own in the chaotic postwar period and repelled several invaders.

De jure recognition was extended to Lithuania by the Great Powers during 1918-1922. On September 22, 1921, Lithuania was admitted in the League of Nations. A permanent democratic constitution was adopted on August 1, 1922.

The most important step in the internal consolidation of Lithuania was the land reform. Within a few years, over 45,000 new farms were established. During the ten-year period preceding World War II, grain production increased by almost 100 per cent. Butter production was raised from 7600 to 19,900 metric tons, and butter export increased from 2051 metric tons in 1927 to 16,386 in 1939.

The number of industrial enterprises grew from 2474 in 1920 to 16,131 in 1939.

Successful efforts were made to insure the health and general well-being of the people. Numerous hospitals were built and community centers opened.

The progress in education during the period of independence can be seen from this table:

	1920	1927	1939
GRADE SCHOOLS:	1173		2716
Teachers	1483		6710
Students	71,648		338,460
SECONDARY (HIGH) SCHOOLS	40		97
Students	9076		26,733
VOCATIONAL SCHOOLS:		7	143
Teachers		50	1591
Students		197	14,040

Eight schools of higher learning were established during the same period.

RELATIONS BETWEEN LITHUANIA AND USSR

After their failure to subdue the young Lithuanian State by force in 1918-20, the Soviets concluded a peace treaty with it on July 12, 1920, in Moscow. According to this treaty Soviet Russia recognized Lithuania as a sovereign and independent State and renounced all claims to Lithuanian territory. Article 1 of the treaty reads:

> In conformity with the right declared by the Russian Socialist Federated Soviet Republic of all peoples to a free self-determination, including the right of full secession from the State of which they were part, Russia recognizes without any reserve the sovereignty and independence of the State of Lithuania

10

with all juridical consequences resulting from such recognition, and voluntarily and forever renounces all sovereign rights possessed by Russia over the Lithuanian people and territory. The fact that Lithuania was ever under Russian sovereignty does not place the Lithuanian people and their territory under any obligation to Russia.

On September 28, 1926, a Non-Aggression Pact was concluded between Lithuania and the USSR, whereby the latter again reaffirmed its guarantee of Lithuanian independence. The pact was reinforced in 1933 by the signing of a convention defining aggression. This provided that "no consideration of a political, military, economic or any other nature shall serve as an excuse or justification for aggression."

All these pledges and assurances, however, proved to be mere scraps of paper. When the deterioration of relations between Nazi Germany and the Western Democracies was reaching its climax in 1939, efforts to include the USSR in the peace front to counter the Nazi-Fascist axis ended in failure. Under the guise of a treaty of non-aggression with Nazi Germany, the USSR joined the Nazi-Fascist conspiracy through the secret agreements of August 23 and September 28, 1939.

II.

LITHUANIA—VICTIM OF THE NAZI-SOVIET CONSPIRACY

> *The colonialists decided to create a puppet government which, posing as an "independent" regime, would in fact obey the will of the colonizers.*
> —NIKITA S. KHRUSHCHEV, 1960

A PERIOD OF THREATS AND PROVOCATIONS

With the outbreak of World War II, Lithuania became a prized objective in the Nazi-Soviet intrigue. As soon as the Nazi forces invaded Poland, Lithuania adopted a policy of neutrality and rigidly adhered to it. Lithuania's neutrality was unacceptable both to the Nazis and the USSR. *Izvestia* wrote this about the neutrality of small states, on May 16, 1940:

> Recent war events (the occupation of Belgium, the Netherlands, and Luxembourg) once again prove that the neutrality of small states, which lack the power to support it, is a mere fantasy. . . . We should once more remind them that the policy of neutrality of some small countries could not be called anything but suicide.

On September 17, 1939, the Red Army crossed the Polish-Soviet frontier and some days later reached the former

12

Lithuanian-Polish administrative line. On September 26, 1939, Molotov, then Commissar for Foreign Affairs, expressed a desire to reconsider Lithuanian-Soviet relations. The negotiations on October 2-10, 1939, in Moscow, were very difficult. The Lithuanian Government was faced with a dilemma: to accept the Soviet demands or to risk a military occupation. Meanwhile, the USSR was concentrating its forces on the Lithuanian frontier. The Lithuanian Government, unable to withstand the immense pressure, was forced to sign the so-called "mutual assistance" pact, which was anything but mutual. In light of subsequent events, it suffices to glance at Article 7 of this pact to grasp the perfidiousness of Soviet policy:

> Realization of this pact should not affect to any extent the sovereign rights of the Contracting Parties, in particular their state organization, economic and social systems, military measures and, in general, the principle of non-intervention in internal affairs.

In accordance with the imposed "mutual assistance" pact, the USSR established several military bases in Lithuania. The first six months passed without important incident. But Moscow's seemingly correct attitude ended soon after the conclusion of the peace treaty between the USSR and Finland on March 12, 1940. At the end of April the Lithuanian Minister in Moscow reported that "a black cat has crossed the road of Lithuanian-Soviet relations." On May 25, 1940, the Soviet Government in a note accused the Lithuanian Government of kidnapping Soviet soldiers. On May 30, 1940, the Soviet Government published a press release "on provocations by the Lithuanian authorities." Subsequent efforts of the Lithuanian Government to satisfy the rulers of the Kremlin were doomed to failure, since the USSR was already methodically implementing its secret agreements with Hitler as to the disposition of Lithuania.

USSR ULTIMATUM AND INVASION

On June 14, 1940, at 11:50 p.m. Molotov presented to the Lithuanian Minister of Foreign Affairs, at that time in Moscow, a Soviet ultimatum which concluded as follows:

The Soviet Union considers that the present situation cannot be continued. The Soviet Government considers it necessary and urgent:

1. That the Minister of the Interior, Skucas, and the Director of the Department of Security, Povilaitis, be immediately delivered to the judicial authorities and tried as directly guilty of acts of provocation committed against the garrisons of the Soviet Union in Lithuania.

2. That a Government be immediately formed in Lithuania capable of assuring and determined to ensure the proper fulfillment of the Treaty of Mutual Assistance between the Soviet Union and Lithuania and to suppress firmly the enemies of this Treaty.

3. That a free entry into the territory of Lithuania be immediately assured for units of the Army of the Soviet Union which will be stationed in the most important centers of Lithuania and which will be sufficiently numerous to assure the enforcement of the Treaty of Mutual Assistance between the Soviet Union and Lithuania and to put an end to acts of provocation directed against the garrisons of the Soviet Union in Lithuania. . . .

14

The Soviet Government will wait for the answer of the Lithuanian Government until 10 a.m. on June 15. Failure to respond at the established time will be considered as a refusal to carry out the above-mentioned demands of the Soviet Union.

The President of the Republic of Lithuania, Antanas Smetona, called for the rejection of Soviet demands. The majority of his Government, however, in order to prevent the destruction of the country, insisted on acceptance of the Soviet ultimatum. On June 15, 1940, large military units of the Red Army poured into the country.

AGGRESSION MASQUERADING AS A LEGAL ACT

According to the Kremlin's plan, the annexation of Lithuania by the USSR was to be carried out not by direct Soviet order, but by "Lithuania herself." For this purpose the Soviet Deputy Commissar for Foreign Affairs, V. G. Dekanozov,* pieced together on June 17, 1940, the so-called Lithuanian "People's Government." This "Government" included some non-Communists who believed that the USSR would honor its promise to preserve Lithuanian independence. Their hope rested on Soviet statements that the aim of the invasion, and thus the cornerstone of Lithuanian-Soviet relations, was the implementation of the imposed "mutual assistance" pact. They nurtured the idea of a new Lithuanian-Soviet friendship pact on new terms.

But on July 2, 1940, the Lithuanian puppet Minister of Foreign Affairs, Kreve-Mickevicius, was summoned to see Molotov, who told him frankly:

---

* Dekanozov was liquidated as one of Beria's men in 1953.

You must take a good look at reality and understand that in the future small nations will have to disappear. Your Lithuania, along with the other Baltic nations, including Finland, will have to join the glorious family of the Soviet Union. Therefore you should begin now to initiate your people into the system which in the future shall reign everywhere.

In order that this "entry into the glorious family" seem proper to the eyes of the world, the "representatives" of the Lithuanian people themselves had to ask to be taken to the bosom of the Soviet Union. Thus the Kremlin ordered the Lithuanian puppet Government to hold "elections" to the so-called "People's Diet." The candidates to the "Diet" were selected without exception by the Communist Party. With the Red Army everywhere, and threats to non-voters in the air, the electorate had no choice but to "vote" for the Kremlin candidates.

Before the "election," neither the electoral platform nor any statement of the puppet Government or of the Communist Party mentioned the incorporation of Lithuania into the USSR. Only after the "election" did the Communist Party launch a campaign which featured slogans demanding that the Stalin constitution be introduced into Lithuania and that Lithuania become a part of the USSR.

On July 21, 1940, the "People's Diet" convened for its first session. At least fifty-eight of its seventy-nine members were Communists. The stage was set for the last act of the burial of Lithuania's independence. Instructions were clear and to the point. One hour and three minutes after the opening of the session, the "People's Diet" adopted the resolution which introduced the Soviet system into Lithuania and declared Lithuania a Soviet Republic. After a brief intermission—because the second resolution had not yet been translated from Russian into Lithuanian—the "People's Diet" gave its unanimous approval to the second resolution, which petitioned the Supreme Soviet of the USSR that Lithuania be admitted into the Soviet Union.

Thus, although the "People's Diet" fulfilled the role assigned to it by the Soviet planners, in no way did it represent the will of the Lithuanian nation. Although the decisions of the "Diet" were carried out in the name of the Lithuanian people, the strong hand of the Kremlin pulled all the strings.

In its report on Soviet aggression against Lithuania, the Select Committee of the United States House of Representatives to Investigate Communist Aggression states that:

> Any claim by the USSR that the elections conducted by them in July 1940, were free and voluntary or that the resolutions adopted by the resulting parliaments petitioning for recognition as a Soviet Republic were legal, — are false and without foundation in fact.

III.

LITHUANIA RESISTS SOVIET AGGRESSION

*The struggle for freedom, when once
    begun
With the father's blood, is bequeathed
    to the son.
Though broken a hundredfold by the
    power of the foe—
Ends in victory.*

—ADAM MICKIEWICZ

THE PROTESTS OF THE PRESIDENT AND DIPLOMATIC REPRESENTATIVES

Lithuanian resistance against the Soviet suppression of Lithuanian independence began on the first day of the Soviet invasion.

In protest against Soviet aggression, the President of the Republic of Lithuania left Lithuanian territory on June 15, 1940, to maintain the struggle for the restoration of his country's independence beyond its borders.

All the diplomatic representatives of independent Lithuania strongly and unanimously condemned the Soviet aggression. They presented their protests against the Kremlin's falsification of the will of the Lithuanian nation to the governments to which they were accredited.

18

The Lithuanian Minister in Washington, D.C., in his note to the U.S. Secretary of State, on July 22, 1940, stated:

> In view of the foregoing, I deem it my duty to register my plea and my hope that the Government of the United States of America, champion of legal intercourse among nations, will consider this present Soviet occupation of Lithuania as an illegal act contrary to the spirit of International Law, and will accord, if possible, every assistance to Lithuanian citizens wherever there are no legal representatives of the Lithuanian State.

In his note to the Minister of Foreign Affairs of Great Britain the Lithuanian Minister in London wrote on the same day:

> In these circumstances, my duty as a representative of the Lithuanian people in this country, is to voice a most solemn protest against this wanton act of aggression against my country. At the same time, I wish to declare that I am unable to recognize as valid and binding any decision of the Parliament elected under foreign domination or any act of the Government formed and acting under duress.

The Lithuanian Minister to the Holy See, in the Vatican, stated in his note to the Secretary of State of His Holiness, on July 22, 1940:

> Under such circumstances, I, as Minister to the Holy See, duly accredited by the constitutional authorities of Lithuania, deem it my honor to state that the resolution of the so-called "People's Diet," which has been imposed by a foreign government, is illegal and completely inconsistent with the will of the Lithuanian people, who will never recognize this violation of its

19

right to be free, independent and sovereign in its own country; to protest publicly against the unprovoked aggression by the Union of the Soviet Socialist Republics, which had violated the treaties, the principles of International Law, and the sovereignty of Lithuania; to ask the Holy See not to recognize the incorporation of Lithuania into the Soviet Union.

Lithuanian diplomatic representatives sent similar notes to the Governments of Argentina, Brazil, Denmark, France, Germany, Hungary, Italy, Portugal, Romania, Sweden, Switzerland, Uruguay, Yugoslavia, etc. Simultaneously, the Lithuanian diplomatic representatives presented their protests against the falsification of the will of the Lithuanian nation directly to the puppet Government of Soviet-occupied Lithuania.

The Lithuanian Minister in Rome stated in his protest:

In view of the resolution of July 21, 1940, passed by the so-called "People's Diet" and incorporating Lithuania into the Soviet Union I declare:

primo: the so-called "People's Diet," constituted under the military occupation, oppression and terror of a foreign country which had broken treaties and principles of International Law and committed an act of aggression, is not a representative body, but a tool in the hands of its oppressors;

secundo: its resolutions do not express the will of the Lithuanian nation, and bind neither the people of Lithuania nor myself, the legal representative of the independent and sovereign state of Lithuania;

tertio: I protest with horror against the treacherous resolution, aiming at the destruction of the independence of Lithuania, which was restored after centuries of sacrifices, devotion and battles.

As long as the hearts of Lithuanians beat, they will fight for the restoration of the old and noble state of Lithuania. The Independence of Lithuania will be restored.

LITHUANIAN PEOPLE'S RESISTANCE

The first conspicuous manifestation of popular resistance against the Soviet rule was the boycotting of the "elections" to the "People's Diet." The Kremlin was most concerned to ensure the greatest possible turnout of Lithuanians to vote for the Soviet-nominated candidates. Intimidation was undisguised: each voter had to present his passport to be stamped at the polls, and those with unstamped passports risked serious consequences. Yet very few people voted on that July 14, 1940.

The next step in the crystallization of popular resistance was the founding of several underground resistance organizations. Among these the Lithuanian Activist Front, formed in October, 1940, was the foremost.

The military and political leadership of the resistance established residence in the city of Vilnius, while Kaunas became the center of its organizational network. Soon all of Lithuania was covered with five-man underground units. The leaders of these "fives" formed additional units, and this structure was followed to the top of the pyramid—the supreme command. The underground organization was composed of Lithuanians of various political beliefs and religious faiths. They were united in their determination to fight against the Soviet intruders and to restore the independence of Lithuania. High school and university students, as well as workers, formed the core of the Lithuanian underground.

21

One of the main aims of the underground was to protect the Lithuanian population from NKVD* provocations. The underground also endeavored to maintain liaison with the free world, and planned to organize an insurrection at a suitable time.

The rapid growth of the Lithuanian resistance movement caused great concern to the NKVD. Gladkov, Commissar of State Security of occupied Lithuania, emphasized in his order of April 7, 1941:

> It is established that counter-revolutionary organizations existing in the territory of the Lithuanian Soviet Republic—as well as individuals among the counter-revolutionary elements—are collecting and striving to procure weapons and cartridges in order to organize armed struggle against Soviet rule.

In his memorandum on "counter-revolutionary leaflets," the Commissar of the Interior of Soviet-occupied Lithuania stated on April 14, 1941:

> From the moment of the establishment of Soviet rule in Lithuania, the counter-revolutionary nationalist element developed an active anti-Soviet movement, using for its hostile subversive work the distribution of counter-revolutionary leaflets

---

* The term NKVD is used here throughout for the convenience of the reader. The predecessors of the NKVD were the CHEKA (Extraordinary Commission), and the OGPU (Special Government Political Administration), which superseded the former in 1922. In 1941 the NKGB (People's Commissariat of State Security) was established to fulfill some of the functions of the NKVD. In 1946 the NKVD and NKGB were renamed, respectively, the MVD (Ministry of Interior) and the MGB (Ministry of State Security). Soon after Stalin's death, in 1953, the MGB was again incorporated within the MVD, and in 1954, state security matters were assigned to the newly established Committee of State Security. The role and character of this infamous institution remain unchanged. It is now called the KGB.

and anonymous papers. In the main, the leaflets called for the overthrow of the Soviet Government, sabotage and the boycott of elections to the Supreme Soviet of the USSR. . . . Mass dissemination of counter-revolutionary leaflets has taken place in all the counties of the Lithuanian SSR.

No greater tribute to the efficiency of the Lithuanian underground organization at that time could have been made.

INDEPENDENCE RESTORED

When on June 22, 1941, Nazi Germany attacked the USSR, a spontaneous anti-Soviet revolt erupted throughout Lithuania. On June 23, 1941, the Kaunas radio station was occupied by the insurgents and a provisional Lithuanian Government was proclaimed. Units of the former Lithuanian Army, incorporated into the Soviet forces, revolted at Vilnius and Varena.

The revolt was an unequivocal reply to Soviet propaganda claims that Lithuanians had voluntarily renounced their national independence and joined the USSR.

Soviet propaganda has tried to label the 1941 revolt as "made in Germany." This allegation, however, is completely false. The revolt was a complete surprise to the Nazi government, which ordered the German military commander in occupied Lithuania not to enter into any relations with the provisional Lithuanian Government and not to help it in any way, but to restrict its activities as much as possible.

The Lithuanian revolt of 1941 offers many analogies with the famous Warsaw uprising in 1944. As did the Poles in 1944, the Lithuanians in 1941 sought to throw off the actual

23

occupying power and to confront the new invaders with the established fact of national independence, restored by popular revolt. The Lithuanian freedom fighters succeeded in achieving this in 1941, whereas the Polish insurgents were circumvented by treacherous Soviet tactics. The provisional Lithuanian Government quickly reestablished the administrative organs of the country.

Yet a genuine Lithuanian government was an obstacle to the Nazi "Drang nach Osten." On July 25, 1941, Hitler appointed Gauleiter Heinrich Lohse as head of the Nazi administration for the German-occupied territories of Lithuania, Latvia, Estonia and Byelorussia.

On August 5, 1941, the provisional Lithuanian Government was forced to discontinue its functions. This marked the end of the first phase of Lithuanian resistance against foreign domination and the beginning of another, aimed at frustrating Hitler's designs for his "New Europe."

IV

LITHUANIA RESISTS INTEGRATION INTO HITLER'S EMPIRE

The entire Baltic area will have to be incorporated into Germany.
—ADOLF HITLER, 1941

"GENERALBEZIRK LITAUEN"

The relations between independent Lithuania and democratic Germany had been friendly. The boundaries between the two countries had been defined in the agreement of 1928. Mutually beneficial trade exchanges were developing. But Hitler's rise to power brought this positive development to a halt and initiated a radical change for the worse. In the design for a thousand-year Reich, Lithuania was merely a small country to be quickly absorbed and digested.

On March 22, 1939, Nazi Germany forced Lithuania to cede the Klaipeda (Memel) region. On September 28, 1939, Stalin and Hitler signed the infamous secret protocol whereby the two dictators divided Lithuania between themselves. A narrow strip of Lithuanian territory near Germany's border was assigned to Germany. When the Soviets occupied Lithuania in 1940, Hitler sold this strip to Stalin for 7,500,000 dollars in gold.

Hitler's designs for Lithuania were formally announced

25

immediately after the Nazi invasion of the Soviet Union. By a decree made public on July 17, 1941, the territory of "Ostland" was created, encompassing Lithuania, Latvia, Estonia and Byelorussia. Thus Lithuania became a "province" of the Reich, a synthetic *Generalbezirk Litauen*.

On August 5, 1941, the provisional Government of Lithuania addressed a protest to the Nazi authorities, charging them with impeding its functions. To this, Hitler's Gauleiters retorted that the Fuehrer had "reserved the final solution for this country for the time after the war."

The last semblance of self-administration in Lithuania was removed by the Nazi decree of August 18, 1941, which annulled the law issued by the provisional Government of Lithuania on the restitution of private property expropriated by the Soviets. This decree placed Lithuania in a situation identical with that during the Soviet occupation. The only change was in the color of the occupying power: from red to brown. The designs and policies of the Soviets and the Nazis were remarkably alike.

A NATION GOES UNDERGROUND

Having extinguished the provisional government of Lithuania, the Nazi occupants tightened their grip on the country. Their aim was to exploit the manpower and the economy of Lithuania to the last drop for the benefit of the Nazi war machine.

The Nazi Gauleiters in Lithuania soon received orders from Berlin to mobilize large numbers of Lithuanians for the German armed forces and for slave labor in Germany's war industry. With much fanfare the Nazi administration issued the first order for the formation of a "Lithuanian SS Legion" to fight beside the Germans on the eastern front. The response of the Lithuanian Resistance Movement followed immediately in the underground press:

> We are fighting for our own interests. No one in the course of history has ever fought to become enslaved and to be deprived of his rights. This is also true of ourselves, and we are therefore husbanding our resources for the coming struggle for our national freedom and for a better future for mankind.

The Lithuanian people responded magnificently. The registration centers remained empty, except for a few cripples who had to be rejected in any case. The Nazi administration avenged itself savagely: all Lithuanian universities were closed and many Lithuanian intellectuals were arrested and sent to the Stutthof "death camp." The population was told that, because of the boycott of the SS legion, the Fuehrer would allot no place to Lithuania in his "New Europe."

Yet the Nazis continued their efforts. The second order of general mobilization was issued for the formation of the "Bau-Batallione" (Construction Batallions) for work outside Lithuania. The underground press again unanimously warned the people: "Stay where you are! No one must leave the country." And the new mobilization was an equally dismal failure.

Berlin was becoming furious; the Gauleiters in Lithuania hurled new threats at the population. New mobilizations were announced. This time 100,000 Lithuanians were to be sent to the German war industries. The comment of the underground press was that:

> Lithuanians must answer this new infamous attempt of the occupant as they answered all previous ones—with a courageous and united NO. All threatened with arrest or persecution must not give up but go into hiding, preserving their strength and life for the restoration of Lithuania's independence.

And again the population boycotted the Nazi orders. The manhunt raids by German gendarmes provoked armed Lithuanian resistance. From the planned 100,000 for slave labor in the Reich, the Nazis managed to bring together only some 8,000.

The greater the failures of the Nazi administration, the harsher became the reprisals. Fifty per cent of the Lithuanian Teachers' Institutes were shut down; the number of high school classes was cut in half. The German language became an obligatory subject from the first grade of primary school. A term of *Arbeitsdienst* (labor service) for the Reich was made a condition for enrollment at a university. Soon afterward, high schools were ordered to drop all students who had reached fifteen years of age and who had not yet served in the *Arbeitsdienst*.

These measures, if enforced, would have meant an irreparable setback to the education of young Lithuanians. Steps were taken to circumvent the Nazi orders. To replace the closed Teachers' Institutes, new extensions were added to those that remained. Parents established classes to replace those closed down in the high schools. The teaching of German was quietly omitted below the fifth-grade level. Universities continued to enroll students as "candidates."

A network of three leading Lithuanian underground organizations—the Lithuanian Freedom Army, the Lithuanian Freedom Fighters, and the Lithuanian Front—encompassed the entire country. Liaison was established with the Western Powers. Chief among the factors contributing to the unusual strength and tenacity of the resistance movement was the underground press. In spite of the immense risk to its printers, distributors, and readers, that press kept the Lithuanian people united in their struggle against the Nazi rule. Eight clandestine newspapers of "general circulation" were regularly published. In addition, scores of local "home-made" sheets appeared in practically every large Lithuanian town.

The alertness and efficiency of the underground press under the most trying circumstances may be judged by the following example. On April 28, 1944, the Nazi administration announced the mobilization of all Lithuanian officers and some classes of privates. On the very next day, April 29, special issues of the underground newspapers advised the people not to comply with the mobilization order.

NEITHER VICTORY NOR DEFEAT

The attitude of the Lithuanian resistance movement at that time toward Nazi Germany, the USSR and the Western Powers has been expressed in the editorials of the leading underground newspapers and in statements of the leaders of the resistance movement.

On the occasion of the second anniversary of the Nazi occupation of Lithuania, one of the leading underground newspapers, *Nepriklausoma Lietuva* (Independent Lithuania), wrote in its editorial of June 15, 1943:

The Lithuanian people have never staked their destiny on the victory of either of the occupying Powers—German or Russian; they are not staking it now and will not do so in the future, since neither the victory of one nor the defeat of the other would solve the problem of the freedom and independence of Lithuania. Lithuania is resolved at the right moment to throw in her forces with those of the rest of occupied Europe, in order to regain a free and independent life and to carry on her creative work for her people and for the peace and happiness of mankind.

When the Nazi administration issued a mobilization order on April 28, 1944, the Supreme Committee for the Liberation of Lithuania emphasized in its appeal to the Lithuanian nation:

> The Germans intended to use our men in the West, in dangerous areas and in the cities of Germany where the (Allied) bombing is going on. In fact, they demand that we should fight not against Bolshevism but against the English and the Americans. In this way our nation would be placed in danger of becoming an enemy of England and America, an enemy of those very countries which recognize our independence and in whose capitals even today are our diplomatic Legations. . . . Adhering to our undoubtedly correct attitude—not to give a single man of our nation to die for interests that are alien to our nation and to our State—we shall husband strongly and with determination our young men for the coming struggle in defense of the freedom of our people and our country. We were, we are, and we shall continue to be steadfast and unbending in this attitude.

The Lithuanian Resistance Movement had its share of trials and defeats. By the end of the Nazi occupation, the

30

Gestapo had succeeded in tracking down most of the leading figures of the underground and sent many of them to concentration camps. In the summer of 1944, the German-Soviet front-line cut Lithuania in half and split the underground organization in two. Yet the Lithuanian Resistance Movement did not disintegrate. The second Soviet occupation in 1944 found the Lithuanian nation better prepared, morally and materially, to resist Soviet colonialism than during the first Soviet occupation in 1940.

V.

LITHUANIA FREEDOM ARMY (LFA) AGAINST SOVIET POWER

*Is life so dear, or peace so sweet, as to
be purchased at the price of chains and
slavery? Forbid it, Almighty God! I
know not what course others may take,
but as for me, give me liberty or give
me death.*

—PATRICK HENRY

WAR BREAKS OUT ON THE AMBER COAST

Truman and Churchill erred when they proclaimed on May 8, 1945, that the war in Europe had been brought to an end. In fact, war was still violently raging on the Amber Coast, in small and peaceful Lithuania.

What led the Lithuanian David to defy the might of the Soviet Goliath? Was not such resistance foredoomed to failure? In answering these questions it must be remembered that the Lithuanian people lacked the hindsight that we possess today. At that time, powerful factors, both rational and emotional, militated for a strong stand against the eastern successors of Hitler's genocide campaign.

The most important of these factors was the vivid memory of the first Soviet occupation of 1940-41. Mass arrests, deportations, terror and murder were returning with the

Soviet tanks. Also important were the strength and vitality of the Lithuanian Resistance Movement, fresh from its experiences against the recently terminated Nazi occupation, and well-stocked with arms.

The behavior of the Soviets upon their reentry into Lithuania strengthened the people's will to resist. Lithuanian men, as during the Nazi times, were rounded up for conscription into the Red Army. The NKVD was busy organizing mass arrests, while the Russian soldiers were given freedom to rape and to pillage.

And, above all, the words of the Atlantic Charter, promising self-determination for all peoples after the defeat of Nazi Germany, did not yet have the hollow ring which they later acquired; the Lithuanian people sincerely believed in its words.

THE LITHUANIAN FREEDOM ARMY

The clash was immediate between small detachments of the Lithuanian resistance forces and the NKVD units trailing the Soviet front army. Yet fully organized military units of the Lithuanian resistance took the field only in the beginning of 1945. These units of the Lithuanian freedom fighters, from a few dozen to several hundred men in size, took shelter in the extensive wooded areas of Lithuania. They were not yet under one supreme command. There was sporadic cooperation; several units would merge for larger operations and then go their separate ways. Organization and strategy were diverse.

Up to the summer of 1945 the best organized armed resistance units had been operating in northern Lithuania.

There, almost all groups of freedom fighters had been merged within the Lithuanian Freedom Army (LFA), and functioned under a joint command. Most of the units in the area were led by officers of the former Lithuanian army.

Those resisting in southern Lithuania soon followed the trend toward unification. On August 25, 1945, leaders of armed resistance in that area met for a conference and adopted a decision to merge all the guerilla detachments in southern Lithuania within a single Tauras district. It was agreed that the smallest group of freedom fighters would be comprised of between six and ten men, and that each detachment would operate only in a definite area. A head-quarters was established, a district commander chosen, and other positions assigned.

The guerilla leaders of the Tauras district then went on to organize units of freedom fighters in other parts of Lithu-ania in the same pattern, with the establishment of a unified command for Lithuania's Freedom Army as an immediate goal. After great efforts and amidst countless obstacles, the headquarters of the LFA was set up in January 1947, in Vilnius.

THE BASIC PRINCIPLES OF THE LFA

The ranks of the Lithuanian freedom fighters were com-posed of people from all walks of life—workers, farmers, employees, students and professional people. For all these diverse elements the LFA was to be the crucible which would mold them into a community of high-principled fighters for their country's freedom. The principles of the LFA Constitution became their code of conduct:

34

The ranks of the freedom fighters are open to Lithuanian men and women, irrespective of age, who have high moral standards, courage and determination; who have never committed any acts against the Lithuanian nation; and who are totally devoted to the liberation of Lithuania. . . .

In his actions, the freedom fighter is always guided by the good of Lithuania, disregarding any personal advantage or profit.

The Constitution also defined the three main categories of the freedom fighters as: active, passive, and supporters. In view of the overwhelming power of the enemy, tight security precautions were defined and a severe discipline codified. Extreme secrecy was demanded; contacts and communications were limited to unit commanders. Treason or refusal to fulfill orders was punishable by court-martial. If captured, freedom fighters were not to surrender alive.

The Constitution also demanded that each freedom fighter use an assumed name. Thus the forests became peopled with names borrowed from nature, from Lithuanian folklore and from history: *Naktis* (Night), *Viesulas* (Whirlwind), *Azuolas* (Oak), *Lokys* (Bear), *Kregzde* (Swallow), *Mindaugas* (Famous Grand Duke of Lithuania).

TRAINING OF LFA CADRES

In 1944-45 the cadres of the former army of Independent Lithuania were quite sufficient to provide leadership for the LFA. Yet the losses suffered in the first two years of fighting against the Soviets, and the expansion of LFA activity, made it necessary to train new cadres. To solve the problem, a special training course was organized for non-commissioned officers.

The first course was given in the summer of 1947, with the participation of seventy-two freedom fighters selected from various units. A special training camp was established in the forest. Extreme security measures were taken, since the training involved participation by the LFA elite, including its commander-in-chief. It was obvious that the NKVD would pay any price to seize such a gathering. After several days of training the site of the camp was suddenly shifted a distance of fifteen miles. The course was completed in only two and a half weeks, yet its results were quite satisfactory.

The second training course for future LFA commanders took place in September 1948. The training camp was camouflaged with the greatest care. The Soviet-type tents were covered with branches on top and with moss on the sides. Other tents were built from young birch trees, bent, joined with rods and overlaid with a thick cover of moss. From a distance they looked like genuine forest mounds. Two half-circle ditches with moss seats in the protecting shade of birch trees formed the auditorium.

This time, however, the local NKVD intelligence was more fortunate. In their customary search for freedom fighters, they noticed the training camp and took it for an ordinary guerilla camp. On the last day of the training program, a detachment of seventy NKVD men surrounded the camp. The approaching NKVD column was spotted by LFA sentinels, and the camp immediately erupted with a burst of machine-guns, automatics and rifles. The NKVD detachment was not prepared for such a violent response, and their ring proved too weak to encircle the freedom fighters. Having lost a good half of their men, the NKVD force retreated to await reinforcements. The freedom fighters lost two officers. At nightfall, after burying their fallen friends, they vanished in various directions, leaving an empty camp for the next NKVD assault.

ARMAMENTS AND SUPPLIES

The weapons of the LFA were both of Soviet and German manufacture. Light weapons prevailed, machine-guns especially: the Soviet "Maxims," PPS and SSV automatic rifles. A part of the LFA armament dated from the time of the anti-Nazi resistance. The two largest sources for arms supplies were the retreating German soldiers and the Red Army's frontal units. As the fighting against the Soviet forces went on, the freedom fighters took special care to collect the arms and ammunition of fallen NKVD men. Raids on NKVD arms depots were organized. Yet the shortage of munitions grew more and more severe.

Before the forcible collectivization of Lithuanian agriculture, LAF units subsisted on voluntary food donations from the farming population. These were supplemented by forays into the warehouses where the Soviet administration kept the grain, meat and fats collected from the farmers. From 1948 on, however, the intensified kolkhoz drive and the general pauperization of Lithuanian farmers made it far more difficult for the LFA to obtain food. The LFA command was compelled to issue an order to individual units advising them to create reserves of grain and fats for a longer period, mainly from the sovkhozes and warehouses for state deliveries. How they acquired such reserves may be seen in a typical raid on a sovkhoz in 1949.

The attack was carried out by an LFA platoon of 47 men. During that day, the freedom fighters thoroughly reconnoitered the sovkhoz and its environment, in order to be certain that no concealed NKVD units were in the vicinity. Next, some thirty farmers with wagons were mobilized. When darkness fell, guards were posted on the roads leading to the sovkhoz, while the majority of the freedom fighters surrounded the sovkhoz itself. Three men drove in one of the wagons to the *sovkhoz* office building. Their task was to prevent the two Russian officials, the only armed men in the sovkhoz, from sounding the alarm. Although the trio spoke good Russian and stated that they were NKVD officers from a neighboring town, the Russians would not unlock the door. Only when the sovkhoz night watchman came to the door, pistol at his back, to verify their identities, did the door open. The two officials were then disarmed and bound. In the warehouses sovkhoz workers were mobilized to fill sacks of grain and load them onto the wagons. Thus some thirteen tons of grain were acquired, together with several cows and hogs, added for a balanced diet. The sovkhoz laborers were paid for their work in sovkhoz grain. By dawn the wagons and the freedom fighters had vanished without a trace. NKVD units in several neighboring regions were dispatched to search, but without result.

Soon, however, as the night guards were reinforced, night raids on the sovkhozes became very difficult. The LFA then switched to daytime raids, some of which were disguised as ordinary criminal holdups, in order to avoid NKVD searches and reprisals. Because thefts were then, as now, a daily event under the Soviet system, this method worked especially well.

CAMPS AND SHELTERS

Until 1948 LFA camps served as homes for some units, in addition to their use as training centers.

The *Vaidotas* platoon during the winter of 1946 can serve as an example of a typical encampment. Deep in the forest, on a slight elevation, lie thirty odd snowdrifts. These are in fact tents, so thickly overlaid with snow that the eye is deceived, even from close up. Their construction is basic' ally the same as that used by Lithuanian herdsmen in the old days to take shelter from rainstorms. Four to six poles are driven into the ground in an oblong of three by four yards. These are connected by wooden strips. The front poles are about one-half yard higher than those at the rear, so as to form a slope. The top and sides are covered with spruce branches; inside, a thick layer of dry spruce cones serves as bed and floor for the men. The only other objects in the shelters are the weapons. Although it is not unbearably cold inside, the faces of the sleepers are covered with frost.

The other most commonly used hideouts were under' ground pillboxes. LFA unit headquarters were usually placed in well-camouflaged underground shelters. A typical one was the headquarters of the *Rymantas* unit. Three yards long, two yards wide, and one-and-a-half yards high, it was built on a farm, under a cobblestone road. It usually housed five men. In the front there were racks for weapons, plank' beds at the sides, and shelves at the end for the radio receiver, the typewriter and the files. The main disadvantage of the pillbox was its poor ventilation: when an alarm was sounded all openings had to be shut, and after a while it became almost impossible to breathe. This underground pillbox served effectively for four years, until the farmer was deported to Siberia.

LFA headquarters usually maintained several underground pillboxes, which they constantly changed. "Reserve" pillboxes were usually located in the forests, while those that were "operational" were as a rule built on farm sites. One such "operational" pillbox, headquarters of the *Vytautas* unit, was installed under a farmhouse which did not have a cellar. The extensive activity of the men of the *Vytautas* unit attracted NKVD attention. After a prolonged surveillance, the NKVD concluded that a pillbox was situated on the farm site. One day a large NKVD detachment surrounded the suspected farmstead and launched a thorough search. With special three-yard long iron pikes they methodically pierced every inch of the backyard, the orchard, the stable, and the barn. Then they went on to measure the dimensions of the house from inside and out, looking for double walls, ceilings and floors. The next step was to tear up the floor of the granary and probe the soil underneath with pikes. Finally they tore out the floor of the house itself, and piked through to the hide-out. Three persons were in the pillbox at that time, one of them a woman, the renowned freedom fighter Pushele. When the three realized that they were discovered, they had no choice but to destroy the documents and themselves, as the pillbox was unsuitable for self-defense. This they did; two anti-tank grenades completed the destruction with such force that not only the ceiling of the pillbox, but also the walls of the house blew apart. The

NKVD was able to discover only shreds of bodies and fragments of weapons.

As the NKVD burrowed more and more deeply underground, tragedies of this kind became frequent. The headquarters of the *Birute* unit, for instance, was installed beneath a farmer's woodshed and housed two men. Since it was quite close to an NKVD detachment, the Soviets suspected nothing for some time, and it took them two years to detect the headquarters. On the fatal day the leaders of the *Birute* unit had gathered in the underground pillbox for a conference. Quietly, a large force of NKVD surrounded the farmstead and ordered the farmer to dig up the soil above the pillbox. A burst of automatic fire was the response from below. The NKVD men destroyed the woodshed with grenades and then began to hurl grenades onto the ceiling of the pillbox, which was covered only by a yard-thick layer of earth. As the underground pillbox had but a single exit, the freedom fighters' had but two choices; that is, to break through a triple ring of the NKVD, or to destroy themselves. Since the former was impossible, the freedom fighters exploded the pillbox and themselves. Although their remains were mutilated beyond recognition, the NKVD pieced and sewed the torn parts together, exhibited the corpses in the public square of the town of V., and forced the local people to file by, demanding the names of the closest relatives of the dead.

A unique category of underground hideout was that of the "archive-bunkers." These were situated close to the district headquarters, very well camouflaged, and protected against floods. It is doubtful whether the NKVD has ever succeeded in locating any of these archives; thus, even today, valuable historic material may still lie safely buried under the earth. In addition to their military activities, the LFA collected data on deportations of Lithuanians by the Soviets, on participation in Soviet elections, on NKVD arrests, and on verdicts of the LFA courts. Of particular value are the secret NKVD orders that were intercepted by the freedom fighters.

When the Kremlin tyrants are brought to face their own "Nuremberg trials," the LFA archive-bunkers will provide important documentary evidence.

LIAISON

In the LFA war against Soviet armed power, with the opposing forces intermingled throughout the territory of Lithuania, the problem of liaison was a matter of life and death for the freedom fighters. The most rapid conveyance of plans and orders of the commanders to various units, the distribution of the underground press to the public, the trans-port of munitions from oversupplied units to those with shortages—all such operations required messengers, not only devoted, determined and able, but also inconspicuous in the eyes of the NKVD.

Women played a unique role in liaison work. Many of their names and exploits, marked with personal heroism, are still alive in the people's memory. There was, for instance, Vaidilute, liaison messenger for the *Dainava* detachment. This small, hunched daughter of a peasant was the embodi-ment of courage and endurance. With little rest, loaded with underground newspapers, she would cover several hundred miles, criss-crossing southern Lithuania many times. Herself weaponless, she also transported LFA arms. No task was too difficult to her, no danger too fearful.

Another extraordinary pair of messengers for the LFA were Rimgaile and Duonute, twelve- and fourteen-year-old sisters. They served as regular underground runners, providing important information about the plans of the NKVD from 1946 to 1948, until they were deported to Siberia with their parents.

Fifteen-year-old Juragis served as liaison-man for a company of the *Zhalgiris* detachment. Season after season, this young herdsman transmitted important information about NKVD troop movements by merely standing at the forest edge, cracking his whip or whistling certain melodies. Only on rare occasions was he called to LFA headquarters.

An unusual liaison-man was the seventy-six-year-old beggar, Arturas. A stick in his hand and a sack thrown over his shoulder, he passed through all NKVD roadblocks. If a zealous NKVD sentry should decide to search him, he would begin to beg for a rifle, "to shoot all the skunks in my cottage that are drinking all my eggs." He delivered many thousands of copies of underground newspapers and fulfilled countless important missions. He died in 1951, undiscovered.

THE ROLE OF THE UNDERGROUND PRESS

The underground press was the nervous system of the LFA. It carried the LFA's views and orders to the population with the greatest possible speed. Another important task of the press was to provide objective international news for the population, which was otherwise restricted to a diet of Soviet propaganda.

The press had two main divisions: periodical publications and non-periodical appeals, reports and posters. The mimeograph, in plentiful supply, was the main printing tool. It was the paper shortage, however, which presented the greatest difficulty. During the first several postwar years, the entire Soviet Union was utterly stripped of paper. Stores had no paper bags or wrapping-paper; customers usually brought their own newspapers in which to carry their purchases. The LFA obtained paper mainly by raids on offices of the Soviet administration.

In 1945-46, the publication of the underground press was centralized. But this soon proved impractical. NKVD forays in the vicinity of the central publishing site would interrupt publication for long stretches. In 1947 the press was finally decentralized and apportioned among the larger LFA units. Each unit then had its own press and an information department, to disseminate LFA publications throughout the surrounding territory. The decentralization proved especially useful, as it lessened the work of delivery and risk to the messengers, and made publication immune to NKVD raids. While an affected unit organized itself in a new location, neighboring units would maintain press coverage for its area.

In addition to the efforts of the LFA, the underground press was also distributed in large quantities by village officials. Some of these did so for reasons of patriotism, others in their fear of LFA punishment. To disseminate the underground press efficiently, they used every means that the Soviet administration placed at their disposal: stamps, envelopes, seals, motor-cycles, etc.

To prevent Communist activists and NKVD men from tearing down LFA appeals and posters, the freedom fighters would attach warnings in Russian. So that these would carry conviction, they planted mines under some posters; thus the tearing down of a poster could result in an explosion. Thus LFA posters remained unmolested in public places until the rain washed them away.

The underground press possessed several foreign radio monitoring sites. Special attention was given to the BBC broadcasts. The LFA also had its "correspondents" in all the main offices of the Soviet administration. Editorials for the underground newspapers were usually written by patriotic Lithuanians living a "legal" life. The main task of the press and information departments of the LFA was to prepare stencils, run the mimeographs and expedite the published product. All this work was usually done by one or two men. They alone knew the printing site and the names of their collaborators. From the printing shop the publications were transported to distribution points, usually at night. Each unit had between four and seven such points. There the publications were taken over by the distributors. If the NKVD managed to apprehend one such distributor, he was able to betray neither the printing shop nor the editorial board, even under torture.

Every LFA unit published at least one issue of its periodical each month, in a circulation of some 1000 copies. The circulation of appeals and posters varied widely between a dozen and several thousand copies.

The LFA press and information departments were also well supplied in their printing shops with forms of personal documentation: birth certificates, passports, draft discharge forms, and travel documents. They also had an ample supply of official seals, stamps, samples of signatures and other items necessary for the manufacture of forged documents. Thus the LFA was able to help hundreds of Lithuanians, from whom the Soviet administration withheld the necessary papers, to leave their hiding places and return to a legal life. Many freedom fighters took advantage of these "document factories" to resume civilian life when the LFA began to demobilize its forces.

WOMEN IN THE LFA

The role of women in the armed resistance movement was not confined to liaison, in which they excelled. As the following episodes show, they equalled the men in determination and courage.

In the winter of 1946 Dalia and Naste, freedom fighters working as nurses in two hospitals of the city of Kaunas, were assigned the task of placing two severely wounded guerillas in their hospitals and of providing them with fabricated records of sickness, in order to avoid suspicion by the hospital personnel. Less seriously wounded freedom fighters were taken care of in LFA "hospitals." Naste was able to obtain a bed for one of the guerillas, but somehow the NKVD learned of this, and guards were placed by the ward door. At risk of her life, Naste entered the ward through an outside window at night, took the patient with her, and safely delivered him to a destination 20 miles away. A reliable physician was immediately called to help the patient who was exhausted by this terrible, unexpected journey. Naste nursed him back to strength in two weeks, when he was ready to return to his unit. On the way, however, their sleigh came under machine-gun fire from NKVD men who were lying in wait. The now recovered patient and three other guerillas managed to jump from the sleigh into a road-side ditch, while Naste was wounded in the legs. Despite her severe injury, she held on to her automatic and continued her fire. Under cover of her bullets the guerillas managed to reach the forests and to escape their pursuers.

The list of casualties of the *Varnas* detachment contains the names of a mother and her two daughters. They cooked and took care of the wounded guerillas. When it came to liaison missions, no danger was too great for them.

Ramune, a messenger attached to the LFA detachment of *Sharunas,* was in an underground pillbox with five freedom fighters when over sixty NKVD men launched a surprise attack. She fought together with the men until the last bullet, then exploded herself together with them.

In the famous battle of Kalnishkiai, eighty men commanded by Lakunas valiantly held their ground against an encirclement of 1000 NKVD troops. At nightfall, with their concentrated fire, some guerillas managed to break through the NKVD ring. Among the sixty fallen freedom fighters was the wife of the commander of the detachment and Miss Aushrele. In the heat of the battle, they took over the machine-guns from the fallen guerillas and did not release the triggers until their last breath. This engagement which cost the NKVD over 400 men, was soon immortalized in a popular song. One stanza of the song goes:

> Braid a green wreath, sister dear,
> Bring it secretly.
> Brother, raise a white cross here,
> In the night, gently.

VI

THE TARGETS OF THE LITHUANIAN FREEDOM ARMY

*Tyranny, like hell, is not easily
conquered.*

—Thomas Paine

GENERAL ATTITUDE OF THE LFA

The command of the Lithuanian Freedom Army never considered as its task the expulsion of the Soviet Army from Lithuania. Therefore all LFA units received strict orders to avoid clashes with the regular army of the USSR. The task the LFA set for itself did not directly affect the presence of the Soviet front army in Lithuania, where it stood as a result of the war between Germany and the USSR.

The operations of the LFA were directed against the Soviet organs engaged in the destruction of Lithuania's independence: the administrative apparatus, the Moscow-manipulated Lithuanian branch of the Communist Party, and the NKVD secret police and its armed forces.

At the same time, the Soviets, in their efforts against the LFA, were anxious not to attract world public opinion to events on the Amber Coast or to create eventual international complications; therefore they attempted to rely solely on the NKVD forces. Only on very few occasions were regular Soviet Army units thrown into the battle.

It must be recalled here that before the liquidation of Beria, the NKVD force in the USSR was divided into the NKVD territorial units, i.e., intelligence personnel, and NKVD troops used by the Soviet government simply as an armed force. The latter had many subdivisions: internal, border-guards, railroad, convoy, operational, or special assignment units. The main adversaries of the LFA were the NKVD intelligence personnel, as well as the operational or special troops.

LFA AGAINST THE NKVD

The war between the LFA and the USSR can therefore be more accurately described as a war between the freedom fighters and the NKVD, one arm of the Soviet power. One of the main and permanent aims of the LFA was to weaken the fighting capacity of the NKVD and to demoralize NKVD soldiers in every possible way. Since it was impossible to fulfill this task peacefully, destructive measures were the only means available. According to data of the LFA command, the losses of the NKVD in its war against the LFA, during 1945-1949, were in the vicinity of 80,000 men. Most of these were killed in NKVD attacks against LFA units.

Nor did the LFA itself let pass many occasions to assault and destroy NKVD forces. One such major raid occurred in February 1948, in eastern Lithuania. LFA detachments, led by Perkunas and Viesulas, devised a plan to attack and destroy the NKVD garrison in the town of U. LFA patrols had ascertained that the local militia would not interfere in any fighting between the LFA and the NKVD, but would instead surrender to the LFA. The NKVD garrison numbered 250 men, against whom the LFA mustered some 120 guerillas. The initial phase of the attack was successful. But when the main NKVD force retreated into their brick headquarters, the guerillas met unexpected obstacles. Anti-tank grenades, meant to destroy the building, failed to explode. Equally unsuccessful was the use of gasoline containers to ignite the building, since these had been punctured by bullets early in the battle. The freedom fighters continued their machine-gun and automatic fire for three hours, but were not able to seize the NKVD building.

Another LFA detachment in eastern Lithuania, led by B., had so demoralized the NKVD units with its continuous attacks that for several months the local Soviet administration was completely inactive.

The LFA avoided attacking sizeable NKVD detachments in larger Lithuanian cities. Instead, groups of two or three freedom fighters would stage surprise raids. By these means they inflicted considerable damage on NKVD forces and, even more, kept them in a state of continuous insecurity. A German, prisoner of war of the Soviets, describes his experiences in 1947 with the LFA as follows:

> Once we were taken to a forest to prepare firewood, in the Shiauliai region. (Shiauliai is the fourth largest Lithuanian city.) At the outskirts of the forest, Russian soldiers stopped us, giving us cigarettes and complimenting us, saying: "Deutscher Kamerad ist gut."
>
> Then they left us to enter the forest alone, themselves retiring to the buildings at the edge of the forest. This Russian behavior was very puzzling to us. But some of our comrades, who had worked frequently in the forest, explained that there were Lithuanian Partisans there. The Russians, fearing them,

never ventured into the forest in small groups. There had been instances when Lithuanian partisans seized Germans working in the forests, armed them and forced them to fight against the Russians. In the summer of 1946 there was a great explosion in Shiauliai. We later learned that Lithuanian partisans had blown up the NKVD office.*

NO MERCY FOR THE COMMUNIST ACTIVISTS

Although NKVD units were the principal targets in the field of battle, they were not the main enemies. Most Lithua-nians considered them as merely blind tools of the Kremlin and, except for the Communist party members among them, did not hold them directly responsible for the Kremlin's crimes in Lithuania. Therefore most of the non-Communist NKVD men taken prisoner were released after an indoctri-nation period and harsh admonitions.

No pity was shown and no justification granted, however, to Russian and Lithuanian Communist activists who were carrying out the Soviet policy of oppression and genocide. From 1945 to 1952, the year of the demobilization of armed resistance,** the LFA put to death about 4000 Communist activists.

Punitive attacks against Communist activists in villages or towns did not usually present many difficulties. It was different with those who lived and worked in the larger towns and cities, under constant NKVD protection. Action there was risky and required some imaginative planning. The fol-lowing are two operations that succeeded.

Communist activists in the town of M., protected by a

_____

* Current News on Lithuanian Situation, Vol. VI, Nos. 7-8.
** Single armed freedom fighters or small groups were still active in 1960.

large NKVD garrison, felt wholly secure and were notorious for their ruthlessness in carrying out Soviet orders. The LFA command weighed many plans to strike a blow against the most vicious among them. At last the task was entrusted to freedom fighter M. and Miss P., the LFA agent in the town.

Miss P. was employed in an office of the Soviet administration. Her good looks and attractive personality had made her quite popular among the leading Communist activists. The plan called for a mock engagement to be staged between freedom fighter M. and herself. The leading Communist activists would then be invited to an engagement party at Miss P.'s apartment.

On the appointed day, M. changed into a new suit obtained especially for the occasion, thoroughly rechecked his two pistols, consumed a large portion of lard to acquire immunity against alcohol and, accompanied by his cousin, left for the town of M. to meet his "fiancee." Several Communist youths were already in the apartment waiting for the party to begin. M. introduced himself as a sports instructor from the city of Kaunas and mimed a happy "bridegroom-to-be" quite convincingly. But the top officials failed to appear at the agreed time, and he began to worry. Finally, three of the four expected important guests arrived, including the Secretary of the CP and the commander of the NKVD garrison. Their lateness had been the result of a previous celebration. Although they had obviously already consumed some vodka, they were quite alert and showered the "bridegroom-to-be" with questions about his work, as well as allegedly mutual acquaintances. It was then that the first shadow of suspicion fell. One of the Komsomol girls at the party had a basketball-playing brother in Kaunas, who kept her up-to-date on sports events and people in that city. She apparently could not recall ever having heard the name of the "bridegroom-to-be." M. noticed a slight shift in the atmosphere. The Komsomol girl began to whisper to the important guests. M. thought he heard the snap of a pistol latch in the NKVD commander's pocket. Quick action was called for. The "bridegroom-to-be" feigned a headache as the result of a surfeit of alcohol, and stepped out into the kitchen. Meanwhile the "bride" invited the guests to pose for a group photograph. She placed the leading Communist activists, as guests of honor, in the center, and left space for herself and the "bridegroom."

The "bridegroom" did not wait long. He returned from the kitchen with automatics in both hands, and opened fire. There was no time for his targets even to move. He hastily collected the weapons of the fallen and fled from the apartment, together with his cousin and his "bride," leaving several Communist youths motionless with fright. Despite the noise of the shooting, no militiamen appeared, and the three conspirators were able to reach their pre-selected place of concealment.

Unfortunately, however, not all raids against the Communists came off so smoothly. In 1950, four freedom fighters were killed in an attempt to liquidate three Communist activists.

In the event that an official of the Soviet administration, not himself a Communist party member, should act to bring special or unusual harm to the population, the case was referred to a special LFA court for a decision. For example,

Prosecutor V. in the region of R. had, in his zeal, deported several hundred Lithuanians to remote regions in Russia, and had executed a dozen civilians as LFA collaborators. At the beginning of 1948 such a court passed a verdict for the liquidation of Prosecutor V. Freedom fighters G.and L. were charged by the LFA court with the execution of the task, but their attempts to reach a position close to the Prosecutor were unsuccessful. Some months later, however, about one thousand passport forms were stolen from a bailiff's office in region R. The Prosecutor decided to investigate personally at the scene of the "crime." The two freedom fighters learned when he was scheduled to arrive at the bailiff's office and disguised themselves as farmers and began to mow the grass in a ditch beside a road where the Prosecutor would pass. Along the road itself they scattered broken glass, so that punctures would force the investigating party to get out of the car.

The plan went off perfectly. Since the punctures occurred within a few hundred yards of the bailiff's office, the Prosecutor and his NKVD guard continued on foot. Their walk led them past the "harvesters," who attacked so swiftly and silently that the driver, left behind to repair the tires, noticed nothing. Only when he finally arrived at the office and discovered his superiors missing, did he sound the alarm. The corpses of the Prosecutor and his guard were found in the roadside ditch, covered with freshly mown grass.

Of course, not all punitive attacks were as successful as these. Many claimed the lives of the freedom fighters who engaged in them.

THE STRUGGLE AGAINST POLITICAL FRAUD

Moscow made its first attempt in 1940 to disguise its aggression against Lithuania as a legal act. The next important move in this masquerade was the announcement of the "election" of the country to the Supreme Soviet of the USSR in 1946. The mock election (see p. 21) was necessary for the Communist propaganda machine in its efforts to mislead world public opinion, which still associates the word "election" with legality.

The LFA opposed the mock elections to the Supreme Soviet because they were a parody of democratic suffrage and a falsification of the people's will. The LFA underground press therefore launched an anti-election campaign to explain the political background of the situation. The population was urged to boycott the election proceedings. LFA units received instructions to prevent Communist activists from terrorizing the inhabitants during the "election campaign." But their most extensive activity was reserved for the eve of the "election," when freedom fighters had orders to:

(a) collect passports from the population, so that those whose passports had not been stamped because of failure to vote could excuse themselves by saying their passports had been seized;

(b) keep NKVD garrison buildings under constant fire, so that they would be less active the next day, because of exhaustion;

(c) cut telephone wires and destroy local traffic bridges so that on "election" day "electoral commissions" and Communist activists would find themselves isolated from the centers and would be unable to visit individual farms with voting boxes or otherwise to terrorize the inhabitants into voting.

Let us take a closer look at some typical election episodes. In district B., an LFA unit took up a convenient roadside position a week prior to the "elections." Several freedom fighters disguised in Red Army uniforms and equipped with binoculars observed traffic on the road. Whenever they spotted an "election" truck or automobile covered with posters and slogans, they stopped it, disarmed those inside, and diverted it, passengers and all, from the road into the forest. During a four-hour period, seven cars with thirty-eight agitators and NKVD men were held up and diverted in this way. The freedom fighters then burned all the "election" propaganda and four of the cars. The Communist activists were executed, while three other cars and non-Communist NKVD men were set free to go their way.

Visiting Communist activists were expected at a pre-election meeting held in the town of K. They were accompanied by a dozen NKVD men. Three miles outside the town they were met by machine-gun crossfire. Their cars ignited, and only a few NKVD men managed to crawl to safety along roadside ditches. Communist activists were largely passive in that district for a long time thereafter.

On the eve of the "election," the clatter of machine-guns and automatics, punctuated by muffled grenade explosions, was heard throughout all Lithuania. The entire country resembled a front line. The Soviet administration, aware of the moods governing the country, threw in all its available forces to make the "election" a success. The entire body of Communist activists was mobilized and an NKVD army,

60,000 strong, was put on a war footing. The territory of Lithuania was divided into 2277 electoral districts. Each district was assigned to a number of Communist activists and between 20 and 30 NKVD men. The polling places were covered with sandbags. Each person entitled to vote received in advance an announcement saying that it was his duty to do so. Special transportation for the conveyance of sick and old people to the polling places was organized in each village. Communist propaganda began spreading the rumor that those who voted before 10 a.m. would be rewarded with vodka and sausage, while those who failed to vote would be deported to Siberia.

Despite the threats and promises, on "election" day most Lithuanian villages were as empty and silent as cemeteries. By noon, not even one per cent of the electorate had cast their vote in most of the districts. As a result, groups of between 5 and 15 NKVD men were sent to the villages to gather votes during the afternoon. As the villagers saw them approach, they would either conceal themselves or quickly leave their homes. Some brave people bluntly told the NKVD men that as Lithuanians they could not vote for a Moscow-controlled government. When the dust had settled, no more than 27 per cent of the electorate had voted, although Communist propaganda claimed a turnout of 96 per cent.

The "elections" of 1947 and 1948 met a similar fate. The boycott was especially effective during the 1947 election to the so-called Supreme Soviet of the "Lithuanian Soviet Socialist Republic." Not more than 15 per cent of the electorate took part, although the organ of the Lithuanian CP, *Tiesa,* claimed in its 1947 issue No. 35 that "the election took place in a very exalted atmosphere" and that "no less than 96 per cent of the electorate participated."

LFA AND THE MASS DEPORTATIONS*

Whenever the Soviets initiated mass deportations from Lithuania, they doubled the strength of their NKVD units. The ratio of power between the LFA and the NKVD then became so unfavorable to the former than any open combat between them would have been suicidal for the freedom fighters. Moreover, the LFA was fully aware of instructions given by Serov, assistant to the infamous Lavrenti Beria, that any attempt to obstruct the deportations must be immediately met with force. Any armed intervention by the LFA would therefore have resulted in the mass murder of those to be deported, blame for which would be attributed to the Lithuanians themselves.

Yet the LFA did not remain a mere passive observer of Soviet genocide. Through its informers in the Soviet administration and in the CP apparatus, the LFA sought to discover in advance the names of those to be deported and the dates of the deportations. Whenever they were able to obtain such information, their duty was to warn the families in danger. This was not easy, as prior to deportations the NKVD network of spies and informers was very much tightened.

---

*Mass deportations from Soviet-occupied Lithuania were carried out on June 14-20, 1941; July-September, 1945; February 18, 1946; July-December, 1947; May 22, 1948; March 24-29, 1949; June, 1949; March, 1950. About 350,000 people were deported to remote regions of the USSR, where many perished under the inhuman conditions of Soviet slave labor camps, Arctic cold, disease, and starvation.

During the deportations of 1948, six freedom fighters of the *Raishupys* detachment hurried from farmstead to farmstead warning the inhabitants of the deportation schedule set for them. The roar of NKVD cars, interrupted by women's screams or a series of gun shots, reached their ears from the places they had just left. Absorbed in their task, the freedom fighters stumbled upon NKVD informers, who sounded the alarm. The freedom fighters took refuge in a brick stable, which was immediately surrounded by some 200 NKVD men. The freedom fighters resolved to sell their lives dearly. The unequal struggle lasted almost three hours. Four freedom fighters were already dead when the remaining two ran out of ammunition. They exploded themselves with a grenade. The NKVD lost thirty men, including the district security chief and two officers.

Another important task of the LFA was to help relatives to protect the property of the deportees from being looted. In such cases the freedom fighters would place mines by the gate of the farmstead and post a warning forbidding entrance. In the beginning, NKVD men disregarded such warnings, but after several mines exploded, the looting of desolated farmsteads decreased.

FREEING OF PRISONERS

The front units of the Red Army, pushing the Germans out of Lithuania, were followed by NKVD detachments, which began immediately the purge of the Lithuanian population. The first wave of the purge was directed against the so-called Nazi collaborators. In NKVD terminology, a collaborator was even a farmer who had delivered to the Nazi administration the compulsory requisitions. This, despite the fact that failure to do so had meant deportation to a Nazi concentration camp. Having dealt with the so-called collaborators, the NKVD apparatus was turned against other "enemies of the people," especially those suspected of collaborating with the "bandits"—the official Communist term for the freedom fighters. Arrests assumed mass proportions. Temporary prisons sprang up in every community. In some places roofless pits served as prisons in which prisoners were held for weeks, until there was a sufficient number for a convoy to the district NKVD office. The next stop was the central prisons in Kaunas, Shiauliai and Vilnius, whence monthly transports of prisoners, in groups of not less than 3000, would depart for the labor camps of Magadan, Vorkuta, Kolyma, and elsewhere in the Arctic region of the USSR.

The LFA was powerless to stop these arrests. It did all it could, however, to obstruct them. The two principal measures were attacks on the local temporary prisons to liberate the prisoners, and death sentences meted out to informers.

In central Lithuania, detachments of freedom fighters even succeeded in reaching NKVD prisons in the cities of Kaunas and Panevezhys. Other units would lie in wait for transports of prisoners and raid them. In some cases assaults were made on NKVD groups as they made their arrests.

In 1947, an LFA detachment commanded by Aras stopped several NKVD trucks loaded with prisoners in K. district. The NKVD men were disarmed and executed, the trucks burned, the prisoners liberated.

61

In 1948, a unit of freedom fighters under Dobilas's command received word that six NKVD men, led by the NKVD prosecutor of district J., were on an orgy of arrests in the village of V. Four freedom fighters, sent to free prisoners, crawled unobserved to the farmstead where the prosecutor was busy at that time. At a favorable moment the freedom fighters caught the prosecutor and two NKVD men with their automatics and felled them. The other NKVD men tried to return their fire, but were silenced by grenades tossed through windows of the house. Six prisoners were set free, and the freedom fighters returned to their hiding place with a machine-gun and two automatics as their booty.

ILLEGAL DRAFT INTO THE RED ARMY

The western half of the country was still in German hands when the Soviets began drafting Lithuanians into the Red Army in the part of Lithuania that they had "liberated." The Lithuanian population considered this draft as illegal as those previously conducted by the Nazis, and boycotted it.

"If I must die, I prefer that it be here, defending my homeland, and not somewhere abroad fighting for a new slavery." This feeling prevailed among the young Lithuanians affected by the draft. Many of the Lithuanian men, whom the NKVD had managed to seize and to outfit in Red Army garb, would take the first opportunity to escape into a forest and join the LFA, with all their arms and equipment.

Yet the Soviet administration surpassed even the Nazis

in their brutal handling of draft evaders. While the Germans would wait several days for the draftees to register, and would only then launch their raids, the Soviets would send out special NKVD units on a combing-through operation on the very day of the draft. Every man who tried to escape the NKVD searchers, was shot without warning. NKVD units would surround barns and spray hay- or wheat-stacks with bullets. In one such combing-through operation in a village in district C., 18 young Lithuanians were killed.

The "draftees" were first placed in temporary prisons, and from there transported to the draft centers in the larger cities. The LFA, then in its formation period, took every opportunity to help those who had been seized. In the district of K., for instance, the NKVD had rounded up a group of young Lithuanians and locked them in a granary guarded by six NKVD men. The freedom fighters managed to get close to the granary unnoticed and to kill the guards with grenades. When an NKVD unit arrived to transport the draftees one hour later, they found a broken door, an empty granary, and six NKVD corpses.

LFA AGAINST SOVIET COLONISTS

In preparing the field for its collectivization, the Soviet administration first attempted to destroy the private system of Lithuanian agriculture. In 1945, individual farmers were already subjected to heavy taxation, heavy compulsory deliveries and labor quotas for the state. The farmers were not allowed to purchase fertilizers and machinery, and were forbidden to hire farmhands.

At the same time, to increase the attractiveness of the kolkhoz system, already existing kolkhozes were exempted from taxes, as well as from compulsory deliveries and labor quotas for the state. Moreover, special machinery and tractor stations were established and put at their disposal. Yet the exploited and persecuted farmers still refused to embrace the kolkhoz system. It was then that the Kremlin imposed its usual tactic—mass deportations.

After the mass deportations of farmers in 1947, 1948, and 1949, many Lithuanian villages were completely depopulated. The Soviet administration then began to settle these with *kolkhozniki* imported from Soviet Russia. Immediately upon their arrival, these colonists dutifully expressed their desire to create kolkhozes. The remaining Lithuanian farmers in such villages who tried to resist collectivization soon found themselves in a convoy, accompanied by the NKVD, eastward-bound to the regions of Krasnoyarsk, Irkutsk, and Vorkuta. Most of the Russian colonists soon proved to be NKVD agents, especially trained for a specific task: the collectivization and Russification of Lithuania.

The infiltration of Lithuanian villages with Russian colonists confronted the LFA with a grave problem. Opinions of the LFA leadership were divided on the subject. Some leading freedom fighters thought that the LFA was not powerful enough to expel the Russian colonists from Lithuanian soil. Others insisted that the LFA must undertake immediate action against the colonization, since the Kremlin's axe, striking at the very roots of Lithuania, threatened the existence of the Lithuanian nation. The latter view was embraced by the majority of the LFA, and action against the colonists began.

How this action was carried out can be seen from the case of kolkhoz A., in the district of V. Most of the inhabitants of the village of A. had been deported for their resistance against collectivization. Their farms were settled by Russian colonists, among whom were fifteen families of especially trained Russian agents. The settlers immediately founded a kolkhoz and undertook to extend it by absorbing the neighboring villages. An LFA detachment of 100 men, commanded by Shturmas, was given the task of liquidating the Russian kolkhoz. The freedom fighters knew that the Russian *kolkhozniki* had two machine-guns and a dozen automatics and pistols at their disposal. It was also necessary to prevent the district NKVD garrison from giving swift aid to the kolkhoz. In order to achieve this, the freedom fighters successfully raided a distillery in the vicinity of the kolkhoz several days before the kolkhoz operation. In the days that followed, the NKVD garrison, aided by NKVD troops from other districts, engaged in combing-through operations in the neighboring forests and suspect villages. The zeal of the NKVD men, who were most eager to recover 300 gallons of alcohol seized by the freedom fighters, was quite genuine.

With most of the NKVD units busily engaged in an alcohol chase, the freedom fighters were free to proceed with their operation against the kolkhoz. Under cover of night, groups of freedom fighters surrounded kolkhoz farmsteads. The resistance of the NKVD-trained *kolkhozniki* was feeble and short-lived. The surviving families of im-

65

ported Russians were ordered to evacuate the kolkhoz and to depart from the territory of Lithuania in one month's time—the usual procedure in such cases. The *kolkhozniki* did not wait that long. The next night, having buried their dead, they left the village with their belongings, without waiting for NKVD help or advice.

Operations such as this undermined the Kremlin's plans for the colonization of Lithuania at the very outset. Today only a limited number of Lithuanian kolkhozes are headed by Russians, most of whom arrived later, during the Khrushchev era.

LFA RESISTS THE "ANTI-KULAK" MEASURES

Very soon after the invasion of Lithuania in 1940, the Kremlin realized that its greatest enemies were the Lithuanian farmers. Therefore, one of the first tasks of the re-imposed Communist administration in 1944 was to break the backbone of the Lithuanian peasantry. Already on August 30, 1944, a decree was published proclaiming the so-called agrarian reform. Officially, the maximum portion of land for each farmer was set at 75 acres. Yet Communist commissions charged with carrying out the reform were given power to reduce the maximum to 12 acres for those farmers who, in the opinion of a commission, were not favorably inclined to the Soviet system. The commissions made liberal use of their power, and their arbitrariness was unlimited.

Whether the farmer was left 75 acres or 12, he still had to deliver a set quantity of grain, meat, potatoes, hay, milk, eggs, wool and flax to the Soviet administration. In the first years, farmers were not paid at all for these compulsory deliveries. Later on, the Soviet administration began to offer symbolic remuneration. Thus, for delivery of a hundred pounds of grain, a farmer was permitted to buy a comb. The "reward" for his entire yearly compulsory delivery was a permission for him to buy one shoe; it took two years to purchase a pair of shoes. Meanwhile, the farmer was obliged to pay constantly mounting taxes for the "use of soil," to purchase USSR federal loan bonds, and to perform three months of unpaid work for the state each year.

Lithuanian farmers were particularly annoyed and angered by the extreme wastefulness of the Soviet administration. Frequently even the seed corn was taken from them, and left in huge piles for days in the open until it rotted. Potatoes were left for the frost. The farmers were bitterly aware that the Soviet administration had forced the back-breaking deliveries on them, not in order to feed the city dwellers, but to pauperize and finally to liquidate the farmers themselves. The LFA reacted forcefully against these "anti-kulak" measures.

The LFA publicly announced that it would mete out severe punishment to those who accepted from the Soviet administration land and cattle which had been seized from farmers with 100 acres of land or less. The Lithuanian population whole-heartedly accepted this LFA order. In 1946 the Soviet administration was compelled to admit openly that this LFA threat had prevented new settlers from taking over hundreds of thousands of acres of seized land from the government.

The LFA eased the burden of compulsory deliveries by

destroying receipts and lists in Soviet agricultural offices, and by bringing over-zealous collectors of agricultural deliveries to a halt. At the beginning of 1945, the *Gelezhinis Vilkas* guerilla unit surrounded 18 NKVD men who were seizing wheat and meat from farmers. They returned the produce to the farmers and executed the NKVD men. From the village the freedom fighters went to the bailiff's office in the neighboring town of S. The freedom fighters then destroyed all lists of deliveries and loans, thus making it impossible for the Soviet administration to determine which farmers were still "in debt" to the state.

The NKVD unit of region L. was notorious for its terrorization of farmers through compulsory deliveries and never-ending state loans. The freedom fighters resolved that the NKVD unit must be destroyed. Since the guerilla forces were not strong enough to attack the NKVD in the town of L. itself, it was decided to lure the NKVD forces from the city and to compel them to fight under conditions favorable to the freedom fighters. In pursuit of this plan, a group of freedom fighters staged a daytime raid against a state farm and brick factory several miles away from the city. The freedom fighters overpowered the NKVD guards, seized the factory funds, as well as provisions from the state farm, and retreated to a nearby forest. At the same time, another LFA detachment, led by Skirmuntas, secretly took positions along the road leading from the town to the state farm. They did not have to wait long. The NKVD garrison, responding to the alarm sounded by the state farm, ran directly into the crossfire of the freedom fighters. Because of their disadvantageous position, the NKVD men were not able to muster serious resistance, and only two managed to escape alive.

In its drive to make the 1948 sale of state loans a success, the Soviet administration first appointed local villagers as salesmen of the state loan bonds. But this practice soon proved fruitless: without difficulty, the freedom fighters confiscated the collected money and destroyed the lists of purchasers of the bonds. Aware that the state loan drive in the countryside was completely paralyzed, the Soviet administration ordered Communist activists and the NKVD to join the campaign. In some regions of Lithuania this led to terror-measures against the farming population. The LFA did all in its power to blunt the terror weapon of the Communist zealots.

In a typical instance, the freedom fighters received reports about the cruelty of the state loan team in region M. Three freedom fighters were assigned to liquidate them. They took cover in the house of a farmer who had not yet purchased state loan bonds, and waited. When the car with the collectors was some forty yards away, the freedom fighters machine-gunned them and killed seven collectors, while the driver escaped with a light wound.

LFA FIGHTS AGAINST COMMUNIST ROBBERIES

A shout for help, a woman's scream, scattered shots, shreds of Russian songs in drunken voices—these were common sounds in the Lithuanian countryside of 1945-46.

"The Ivans are at it again," was the usual comment of the peasants.

It was a custom of members of the NKVD operational troops to enliven their free time by making "visits," in groups of threes or fours, to the villages. In farmsteads where there were men, the visitors were content to demand brandy and snacks. But when they came to a farmstead peopled only by old men and women, they would herd them all into one corner of the room and, while one soldier kept watch outside, the others would proceed with their "search." All the better items of clothing, shoes, meat, money and watches would end up in the "visitors" sack. On their departure they would fire a salvo of shots.

Such forays by the NKVD encouraged local criminal elements, and the life of the peasants became very insecure. The NKVD commanders and the Soviet administration regarded these robberies as a form of "anti-kulak" activity, and took no real measures against them. In many villages the peasants installed special gongs to warn of the appearance of unwanted visitors. Yet this warning system was not enough to keep the plunderers away, and the intervention of the LFA became necessary.

The villages of the region G. were being terrorized by a well-organized group of NKVD marauders. They even began to murder peasants who refused to obey them. The local LFA unit assigned six freedom fighters to liquidate the robbers. When a scout of the LFA informed the group that four NKVD marauders were "visiting" a farmstead, the freedom fighters crept unobserved to the farmstead and surrounded it. The NKVD men were told to leave the cottage, but they answered with their automatics. The freedom fighters then ordered the farmer's family to leave the room,

and tossed grenades in through the windows. All four robbers were killed, and only one freedom fighter was wounded.

The action of the LFA proved quite effective, and soon
the epidemic of robberies was brought to a halt.

LFA AGAINST MOONSHINERS

Alcohol is an integral component of the Soviet system,
and excessive drinking might be called the main characteristic of the transition from "socialism" to "communism." The
incessant terror, constant insecurity and endless nervous
strain increased the consumption of alcohol in Lithuania to
a dangerously high degree. Under the influence of alcohol,
the people began to forget the need for caution; tongues
loosened, and many families ended up in Siberia because of
a word or two uttered in intoxication against Stalin or the
Soviet administration. The wave of alcoholism affected the
freedom fighters as well, and resulted in a loss of discretion
and displays of unnecessary boldness. Alcoholism amidst the
population and in the underground became inter-related.

Faced with this situation, the LFA command had to take
steps against the excessive manufacture and consumption of
alcohol. In the spring of 1946, the LFA published an order
forbidding the brewing and consumption of illegal liquor.
First offenders were punishable with fines of up to 1000
rubles, while the second offense drew a corporal punishment.
These strict measures soon led to a decrease in the number
of moonshiners and the extent of alcoholism in Lithuania.

✓　　✓　　✓

As the preceding pages show, LFA armed resistance was

71

mainly directed against these aspects of Soviet policy in occupied Lithuania:

(1) the destruction of Lithuania's sovereignty, the political rape of the Lithuanian population, the falsification of the Lithuanian people's will by mock elections, and the illegal conscription of Lithuanians into the Soviet army;

(2) the genocide of the Lithuanian nation—mass deportations, mass arrests, mass importation of Russian colonists;

(3) the economic pauperization and moral degradation of the Lithuanian people—expropriation of farmers, exploitation of workers, rapine and violation by the NKVD; moonshining, alcoholism, and the loosening of morals.

The activity of the LFA was successful to such a degree that for several years the colonial imperialism of the Kremlin in Lithuania was checkmated. The Communists themselves were compelled to admit this. Until 1957, they tried to bury the Lithuanian war of resistance in silence. Yet on December 22, 1957, the deputy chairman of the "State Security Committee" of occupied Lithuania, L. Martavicius, stated that the LFA "had seriously obstructed peaceful Socialist construction."*

---

* *Komjaunimo Tiesa*, Vilnius, December 22, 1957.

VII

SOVIET MEASURES TO ANNIHILATE THE LFA

Whatever wars of extermination the colonialists should wage, the peoples fighting for their liberation will be victorious.
—NIKITA S. KHRUSHCHEV, 1960

SUSLOV—THE KREMLIN'S EMISSARY TO PACIFY LITHUANIA

According to the official version of the Kremlin, the LFA war against the USSR was merely a desperate gesture by a handful of "nationalist bandits." This version, however, was demonstrably false in view of the scope and intensity of the means applied by the USSR to destroy the LFA. The appointment of M. A. Suslov as the Kremlin's special emissary "to pacify Lithuania" is sufficient proof of the nation-wide character of the Lithuanian resistance movement.

Suslov is today one of the world's top Communist figures and scarcely needs an introduction. He had been Stalin's protegé since 1931. In 1933-34, he directed the purges of the Communist Party branches in the Urals and Chernigov (Northern Ukraine). He became a member of the CP Central Committee in 1944. During World War II he led the

Soviet partisans in the Stavropol province, and his expert knowledge of guerilla warfare made him a perfect choice for his Lithuanian appointment.

In 1944, this Communist theoretician, ascetic and fanatic went to Lithuania on Stalin's order. He was officially appointed head of the "organizational bureau" for Lithuanian affairs. The fact is that he assumed control of the entire political, administrative and economic life of Soviet-occupied Lithuania. Any orders or directives issued by this Stalinist Gauleiter were automatically obeyed by the Soviet administration in Lithuania. Suslov's chief aim was to build up the apparatus of the Lithuanian Communist Party as a local instrument for the implementation of the Kremlin policy, and to liquidate the rapidly growing Lithuanian armed resistance—the LFA.

Suslov was able to achieve in some measure the first part of his task. By the spring of 1946 the apparatus of the Lithuanian Communist Party was in motion. Since Suslov was not able to muster enough Lithuanian Communists who were completely devoted to the Kremlin, he had to fill most of the posts with imported Russian Communists. But Suslov was far less successful with the second part of his assignment—the liquidation of armed resistance in Lithuania. When in 1946 he transferred his functions to the newly cemented body of obedient functionaries of the Lithuanian Communist Party, the LFA was much more effective than upon his arrival in 1944. The "pacification" of Lithuania is not found in the long list of Suslov's services to the Communist cause.

CONFESSIONS OF A COMMANDER OF THE NKVD FORCES AGAINST THE LFA

A very interesting eye-witness testimony on the Lithuanian armed resistance by a former NKVD Lieutenant
Colonel, G. S. Burlitski, can be found in the report of the
Select Committee of the U. S. House of Representatives on
Communist Aggression. In his testimony before the Committee, on June 28, 1954, Burlitski answered the following
questions:

Mr. McTigue (Committee Counsel): . . . The Lithuanian
bandits, or the partisans, were fighting the Communists and
had been very effective; is that correct?
Burlitski: Yes.
McTigue: They had become so effective, as a matter of fact,
that the Kremlin lost patience with the whole operation in
Lithuania; is that correct?
Burlitski: Absolutely correct.
McTigue: And in losing its patience the Kremlin decided
to send into Lithuania its top man, Kruglov*, to enforce the
(Soviet) laws or the operation in its most stern manner; is
that correct?
Burlitski: Correct. . . . On a very dark September night
(1944), in the city of Panevezhys, Kruglov called in a top-
secret operational meeting. . . . At this meeting Kruglov sum-
marized the results of the fight against the so-called bandit
movement in Lithuania and said that up to the present time
the measures which had been undertaken had not proven to be
realistic, that the Politbureau of the Soviet Union and Stalin
and Beria themselves were not satisfied with the results. . . .
He ordered us not to spare any efforts and to spend any money

---

* NKVD General Kruglov at that time was deputy to Beria. In 1953
he succeeded Beria.

to create an agents' net, to find out the base and the leadership of the so-called bandit movement. . . . He also ordered that the (NKVD) troops become more active in their fight against so-called bandits. He ordered them to comb through the forests, through the clearings, in forests, villages. . . .

Yet Beria's deputy Kruglov found it as difficult to destroy the LFA as had Suslov. On this we have the word of the same NKVD Lieutenant Colonel Burlitski, who after five years was again sent to Lithuania in 1949, again to fight the LFA. In his testimony to the Select House Committee, we read:

During 1950-1951 the entire battle against the "bandit" movement in Lithuania was entrusted to two NKVD divisions, so-called divisions for special tasks—the 2nd and the 4th Special Tasks Divisions. The headquarters of the 2nd Special Tasks Division was located at Vilnius, and the commander was General Vetrov; and the 4th Division for Special Tasks was located in the city of Shiauliai, and the commander was General Pyashov. These two divisions, under the command of the Generals I just mentioned, were actually doing all the work and all the fighting against the so-called "bandit" movement in the territory of the Socialist Soviet Republic of Lithuania, of course, in connection and cooperation with the local units of the NKVD. In 1949-1951 from members of these two divisions which I have just mentioned, there were many occasions when soldiers, sergeants and even officers, in fulfilling their horrible tasks given them by the government, deserted as a sign of protest. These soldiers half-heartedly obeyed the orders to comb through the various forests in search of the "bandits." They called the combing-through operations *gosudarstvennaya provyerka* (official examination) and did not consider them worth risking their lives for.

"EXTERMINATORS" AGAINST THE LFA

To avoid international embarrassment, the Kremlin endeavored to mobilize Lithuanian Communists against the LFA, and thus to transform the LFA-USSR war into civil strife. In pursuit of this new policy, decreed by Stalin, Suslov and Kruglov began to organize new forces. The Soviet administration called this force "defenders of the people," while the NKVD used the title of *istrebiteli* (exterminators). The population, which had always felt an aversion to official titles, coined its own derogatory term from the Russian word —*stribai*.

In the fall of 1944, even some non-Communist Lithuanians joined the ranks of the "exterminators," thus hoping to avoid being drafted into the Soviet army. But when the Lithuanian underground press and special LFA proclamations disclosed the real aims of the newly organized "exterminators," non-Communist Lithuanians staged a mass desertion from those troops. By the spring of 1945 the "exterminators" were composed merely of Communist activists and criminal elements, who found membership in the new force a useful cover for their rapine. As a military force, the "exterminators" had little impact, not only because they were poorly armed (with plain rifles), but also because they were very much hated and treated as renegades by the population. Nor did the distrust shown them by the NKVD help their morale very much. Neither Suslov nor Kruglov had much confidence in the Lithuanian Communists, and only Russian NKVD men were appointed leaders of the "exterminator" units.

In the field of battle the "exterminators" constantly tried to disengage themselves from the LFA. When the freedom fighters destroyed several detachments of "exterminators" in position at the edge of a forest to spy on LFA movements, their demoralization was almost complete.

The great losses suffered by the "exterminators" are indicated in this article in the September 1960 issue of the Lithuanian Komsomol magazine *Jaunimo Gretos*:

> After the war Pranas immediately joined the defenders of the people. This was in mid-September, 1946. Together with 26 Soviet activists*, he travelled to the environs of Lenkimai, in the bailiwick of Skoudas. They conducted a meeting of farmers and at sundown started homeward. . . . But as soon as their truck reached the forest edge, bandits (freedom fighters; Ed.) opened fire from ambush. The activists tumbled out, took up positions in a roadside ditch, and began to return fire. But the bandits' positions within the forest edge were more favorable, while the activists were exposed in the open field. Here the activists Zhiemelis, Juodis and Konchius fell pierced by bullets, while the Communist youth, Shvelnys, Tauchius, Dimas, and the Communist Stainys, lay wounded.

NKVD PROVOCATEURS AS "FREEDOM FIGHTERS"

The first units of NKVD agents appeared in the summer of 1945. A detachment of "freedom fighters" suddenly appeared in the forest of K. and through the local inhabitants

---

*When Communist activists went to villages to terrorize the farmers for unsubmitted deliveries, non-purchase of state loans, or refusal to join the kolkhozes, they were always accompanied by a large group of "exterminators."

attempted to make contact with the local LFA command. Some of the villagers, who were not cautious enough, led the unknown "freedom fighters" to the LFA unit commanded by Shvyturys. At a pre-arranged time several agents visited the freedom fighters' camp and invited Shvyturys as well as other officers of his unit to pay a visit to their camp "several miles away." Three of the twelve officers of the unit of Shvyturys were suspicious and refused to go. But the other nine, including Shvyturys himself, departed with the guests. Shortly afterward, a series of automatic shots were heard from the direction in which they had left. The Shvyturys unit immediately retreated into the forest. Within some hours, the camp-site was surrounded by a strong NKVD force. Upon finding the area deserted, they arrested and executed the peasants who had trusted the provocateurs, and combed through the forest. Two weeks later the freedom fighters found the corpses of their commander and the other eight officers.

In 1946, a special unit headed by NKVD Major Sokolov went into action. Its task was to form groups of fictitious "freedom fighters" and thus to demoralize the LFA. The Sokolov agents wore the uniforms of fallen freedom fighters and the insignia of their units. They would enter people's homes with the story that they were freedom fighters who had lost touch with their units and who wished to contact the local LFA detachment. To gain the confidence of the population they would sometimes liquidate some of the local Communists, carefully choosing those who had become unreliable to the Kremlin. In some cases, when people who lived close to the forests denied any knowledge of the freedom fighters, the impostors accused them of collaboration with the NKVD and threatened them with execution.

One group of the Sokolov "freedom fighters" even staged a battle with an NKVD unit, during which the NKVD killed two "freedom fighters" and exposed their corpses in the local public square. It was later discovered that the two corpses were executed prisoners dressed up in LFA uniforms.

The Sokolov agents were rarely successful. The LFA command issued strict warnings to the population to distrust all unknown freedom fighters, however authentic they might look or sound. The freedom fighters were ordered always to be accompanied by an associate known to the people they were to visit. This, of course, greatly burdened the movements of the freedom fighters, but there was no alternative if they were to avoid Sokolov's trap.

THE AMNESTIES

In February, 1946, the Soviet administration made public the first Kremlin amnesty for Lithuanian freedom fighters. Leaflets were widely distributed, urging the guerillas to leave their hiding places and to surrender with their weapons to the nearest NKVD units. The leaflets assured the freedom fighters that they and their families would be spared persecution and punishment, provided that they voluntarily left the LFA.

This manoeuvre of the Kremlin gave the LFA command more concern than the "exterminators" and Sokolov's agents together. The LFA command was faced with a dilemma: to permit freedom fighters to take advantage of the amnesty, or to forbid it. LFA leaders had no illusions that the Kremlin would show pity to its enemies, especially those who rose in arms against its imperialist policies in Lithuania. It was obvious that the freedom fighters who accepted the amnesty would be subjected to NKVD interrogation about LFA commands, organizational data, armaments, messengers, collaborators, etc. . . . And if they wished to survive, they would not be able to hedge and pretend that they knew nothing.

Yet the LFA command was also painfully aware that the LFA units would not be able to avoid annihilation by the NKVD indefinitely. Everyone knew that sooner or later it would become impossible to provide the LFA units with arms, food and shelter. The larger LFA units were also vulnerable to infiltration by NKVD agents and provocateurs, and to slow demoralization. Moreover, the international situation gave no grounds for hope that the western democracies, having destroyed the Berlin-Rome-Tokyo axis, would turn their military power against the tyranny of the Kremlin.

After exhaustive and soul-searching deliberations, the LFA command resolved to leave the decision to each individual freedom fighter, with the exception of those whose connection with LFA units had not yet been established by the NKVD. Those in the last category were warned that by accepting amnesty they would harm their relatives and friends. All LFA units were given orders to undertake the following measures with regard to the decision to accept amnesty: (1) to isolate "amnesty-seekers" within the unit for at least one month, so that at the time of their departure they would be unfamiliar with the future situation of the unit; (2) to arm them with the most inferior weapons of the LFA unit; (3) to rehearse them for the impending questioning by the NKVD.

Later events proved that the LFA decision was a right one. Although the number of freedom fighters decreased, the LFA units became more mobile, more united in spirit, and better able to resist NKVD snares. Problems of arms and food supplies were considerably eased, at least temporarily.

The freedom fighters who surrendered to the NKVD eventually became victims of mass deportations together with their families, except for a handful who became collaborators of the NKVD.

NKVD ONSLAUGHT ON THE LFA

The amnesties, the false "freedom fighters," the units of Communist activists and the "exterminators"—all these were but auxiliary means in the NKVD war against the LFA. The main instrument in this process of destruction was that of the armed forces of the NKVD. Several NKVD divisions were spread throughout the entire territory of Lithuania for this purpose. They were assisted by numerous so-called territorial units or detachments of the NKVD. The NKVD operations against the LFA were twofold:

(a) constant surveillance of the population, and upon any indication of LFA activity, detection and encirclement of their headquarters with superior forces, and destruction;

(b) "combing-through" operations in specific areas of Lithuania, i.e., checking the identity of each inhabitant, searching all homes, fields and forests, and destroying any LFA units discovered.

REGULAR SOVIET ARMY TROOPS AND LIGHT ARTILLERY AND PLANES IN THESE UNDERTAKINGS

The outnumbered LFA units engaged the enemy forces only when they were unable to retreat unnoticed. Since the freedom fighters never surrendered, the fighting was always fierce.

In October, 1945, NKVD troops surrounded an eighty-man LFA unit in the village of B., adjacent to a forest. The freedom fighters, who had 21 machine-guns and who were positioned along a one-mile stretch, opened fire first. The NKVD plan was to break through the LFA trenches before nightfall and to split the guerillas up. The battle lasted for several hours, and at dusk the freedom fighters still held their ground. Under cover of darkness, the LFA unit managed to slip out of the encirclement undetected.

In another instance, the P. unit of freedom fighters had settled in a swampy area. Successful raids of the guerillas in that region had convinced the NKVD that the camp of the "bandits" must be in the swamp itself. One morning in August, 1946, the freedom fighters awoke to discover that the entire swamp area was surrounded by NKVD forces. Soon concentrated artillery fire descended on them and continued for several hours. After this barrage, NKVD rowboats began to work in toward the center of the swamp. Only then did the freedom fighters open fire. At nightfall the fighting grew quieter, and the freedom fighters took the opportunity to slip through the NKVD lines by using secret paths known to them alone. Seventeen freedom fighters and over 200 NKVD men fell in that battle.

Sometimes the fate of an LFA unit hinged on a split-second decision, or sheer luck. Just before Easter, 1946, a sizeable NKVD detachment stumbled upon the trail of the *Viesulas* unit in the district of Trakai. When the freedom fighters realized that they had been discovered, there was only one way left to escape unnoticed—across a flooded river. The freedom fighters managed to cross the river with only a few casualties, but hardly had they touched the other shore when they were spotted by an NKVD supply column. The NKVD men mistook the freedom fighters for Russians and started shouting: "Rebyata syuda. Vozmite munitsiyu." (Come on, boys. Get your ammunition).

It was a critical moment. The guerillas instantly realized that if the "rebyata" failed to answer, the supply column would recognize them and cut off their retreat route. The commander of the LFA unit acted quickly and sent six men dressed in Russian uniforms to the supply column. In half an hour, two truckloads of NKVD ammunition were in the hands of the freedom fighters.

Once a unit of the NKVD troops, furnished with trained dogs, was sent into a forest where freedom fighters were reportedly hidden. After crossing the forest, the NKVD men noticed that their dogs had disappeared without a trace. They heard no barks or howls; their signals to the dogs brought no response. The following morning, to the astonishment of the local inhabitants and of the NKVD, the dogs were found hanged.

But fortune does not always favor the just or the out-

numbered. In January, 1946, for instance, the NKVD surrounded an LFA unit commanded by Arlauskas, in a forest.
The fighting was long and fierce, but the freedom fighters
were unable to break through the NKVD ring, and they were
annihilated. One month later the NKVD encircled the camp
of an LFA unit commanded by Meilus, in northern Lithuania. The camp was situated on a wooded hill. Its defense
positions were well laid out, and the freedom fighters had
a plentiful supply of ammunition. The battle lasted two days.
Wave after wave of NKVD troops surged against the LFA
positions, but could not break through them. Only when
Soviet army tanks joined the battle did resistance collapse.
The toll of the battle was 73 guerillas and about 300 NKVD
men.

The NKVD installed secret observation posts along the
fringes of the Lithuanian forests. The homesteads of suspect
farmers were kept under a constant surveillance which was
particularly intensified during the religious holidays, as the
NKVD was well aware of the Lithuanian custom of family
reunions on holidays. The LFA command forbade its men
to visit relatives at such times, yet some freedom fighters still
ventured out, despite the danger and the prohibition.

In one case, five men of an LFA unit commanded by Ainis
went to visit their relatives in their native village. They were
immediately surrounded by thirty NKVD men who were
waiting in ambush. Four freedom fighters fell in the fighting,
while the fifth, although wounded, managed to break through
the ring and to escape. The NKVD, however, followed his
bloody trail to his hiding place and killed him there.

DESECRATION OF DEAD FREEDOM FIGHTERS
AND THEIR GRAVES

In the first years of the Lithuanian resistance war, the NKVD usually left the corpses of fallen freedom fighters untouched. The population could then bury them in the nearest cemetery, or in a common grave at the death site. Such graves were usually surrounded by a fence and marked with a cross. But in the spring of 1946, the NKVD received orders to deliver the corpses of the guerillas to the NKVD garrisons. Then the corpses were exhibited in public squares, and the non-Communist population was ordered to identify them. There were instances when a father would recognize his son, a wife her husband, a sister her brother. Frequently the dead freedom fighters served as outlets for NKVD sadism. The corpses were bridled with the rosaries found on them; prayerbooks were stuffed into their mouths. Other corpses were stood up and supported by sticks, their mouths filled with dung; or the Lithuanian coat-of-arms was carved into their foreheads.

The LFA was not able to protect the corpses of its fallen men from profanation and sadism. In some cases, however, the corpses were stolen or covered with flowers.

Having used the corpses of the freedom fighters for its purposes, the NKVD would bury them in still open war trenches or in some other remote place. The Lithuanian population almost always discovered these burial places, built fences around them, and erected crosses. On Lithuanian national holidays and on All Saints Day, the graves of the freedom fighters were, and still are, adorned with flowers.

Such demonstrations of Lithuanian solidarity with the freedom fighters were a major irritant to the Soviet administration. To prevent such expressions of homage to the fallen freedom fighters, the Soviet administration ordered the graves "levelled with the earth." Local Communist activists and NKVD party members eagerly complied with the order. To curb this vandalism, the LFA mined the graves of the freedom fighters and posted warnings against tampering with them, in Russian and Lithuanian. The mining did much to cool the zeal of the vandals.

✦ ✦ ✦

The various means taken by the USSR to annihilate the LFA had a twofold effect on the freedom fighters.

On the one hand, as the LFA suffered great losses, it became less and less possible for it to function; hundreds of thousands of Lithuanians, suspected of sympathies for the LFA, were deported to concentration camps in the Arctic.

On the other hand, however, the savagery of the NKVD hardened the resistance of the LFA and of the entire Lithuanian nation, deepened national solidarity, and imbued the younger generation of Lithuanians with a yearning for freedom and independence which will be passed on to generations to come. The legend of the freedom fighters is growing stronger from year to year in occupied Lithuania. The Communists may level their graves, but even Soviet totalitarianism is powerless to eradicate their memory from the consciousness of the Lithuanian people.

In a prayer-book written by Lithuanian deportees in Siberia and in 1959 smuggled out to the West, we read:

Martyrs of our nation,
Find wisdom, strength and unity for the laborers
    of our nation.
Find an endless, bright repose for those who lay down
    their lives for their native land.

VIII

THE LITHUANIAN FREEDOM ARMY
AND THE WEST

We ask you in the name of all that is
dear to you, we ask you to help us.
Do you not think that those who have
died for liberty, our beloved ones who
are silent, accuse all those who could
have helped and who did not help?

—Free Radio Rakoczy, Hungary,
November 7, 1956

LIAISON WITH THE WEST

From the moment the Iron Curtain sealed off Lithuania completely, one of the main endeavors of the LFA was to maintain constant liaison with the West.

Radio receivers were part of the equipment of each LFA unit. All western European broadcasts were closely followed, especially those of the BBC.

In 1945, the LFA command succeeded in establishing contact with Lithuanian displaced persons' organizations in Great Britain, France, Sweden and Germany. Representatives of the underground managed to visit their compatriots in the West, and Lithuanian DP messengers crossed the border into their homeland. These trips across the Iron Curtain were especially difficult, since Lithuania shared no borders with the free world. The Lithuanian coast and the Baltic sea were under such tight Soviet guard that it was virtually impossible to escape the country by water. Thus the principal route of the LFA liaison-men to the West crossed the Polish border directly from Lithuania or through the so-called Kaliningrad region (formerly East Prussia).

Although Poland is a satellite of the USSR, the border between Poland and other countries under Soviet occupation has its own Iron Curtain: special border areas with a half-mile wide "death zone," barbed wire fences, watch-towers, trained dogs, and all the other usual paraphernalia. This is how one LFA liaison-man describes his journey from occupied Lithuania into Poland:

> We said our farewells on the night of December 15, 1947. . . . That night we had to cover a distance of 27 miles. Soon we noticed footprints in the snow: some 18 MGB men had crossed our path. . . . We reached a village where a new group of guides was supposed to be waiting for us. . . . Our present guides turned back, while the six of us proceeded to the former Lithuanian-German border. To pierce the Iron Curtain this time we selected a path through East Prussia. We calculated that the East-Prussian-Polish border would be less closely watched than the Lithuanian-Polish border. . . . According to our plan, we had to reach the Rominta river, close to the Russian-Polish border. On December 21, after a seven-day journey, we were marching through a ravine, when we sighted trenches and a barbed wire fence some forty yards away. This was a new Russian-Polish border. We swiftly leaped over the ditches, but the barbed wire fence took more time. . . . We were spotted by bolshevik skiers. . . . We advanced. . . . A Russian unit sped in to bar our road. . . .

In the ensuing clash, three freedom fighters were killed, but the remaining three reached Poland. Yet their worries were not over—they still had to cross the second Iron Curtain, either across the Baltic to Sweden or through Soviet-occupied Germany into West Berlin.

LFA FAITH IN THE WEST

The LFA command, in its evaluation of the international situation in 1945, refused even to consider the possibility that the western Great Powers would fail to oppose Kremlin plans for world domination, and would permit the imposition of Soviet colonial rule on East-Central Europe. The Atlantic Charter was regarded by LFA leaders as an actual blueprint for the postwar world, and not what it later proved to be—a wartime propaganda statement. Moreover, the LFA command was firmly convinced that the security of the western democracies made it imperative for them to bring immediately into play their superior military power against the efforts of the Kremlin to impose Soviet totalitarianism on all mankind.

"We did not believe that the West would fail to continue its struggle for freedom and for human rights; the struggle for which so many noble westerners had shed their blood," wrote one of the LFA leaders.* "We were pervaded with a fighting spirit, eager to contribute to the destruction of the newly emerged enemy of freedom . . ."

This belief in the inevitable strong stand of the West against Kremlin designs for world domination had literally

---

* J. Daumantas, *Partizanai uz Gelezines Uzdangos* (Partizans Behind the Iron Curtain), p. 46.

hypnotized the LFA command. Even the Lithuanian liaison-men from the West, who brought direct and sobering information on the international situation, were unable for some time to shatter that belief.

Faith in the West was especially strengthened when news of the atom-bomb reached Lithuania. August 6 and 9, 1945, (the days of the raids against Hiroshima and Nagasaki), were days of great hope for the LFA command. A special meeting to discuss the international situation took place on August 20. The participants listened with the greatest interest to the BBC report on the power of the atom-bomb. All were convinced that the new era of science would initiate a policy of strength against all aggressors.

The explosion of the first atom-bomb evoked lively discussions among freedom fighters throughout Lithuania. The consensus was that the West would confront the Kremlin with an atomic ultimatum and compel the Soviets to free the captive countries. Suddenly a free Lithuania, and the end of a life of want and endless conflict, seemed almost at hand.

IN THE ABSENCE OF AN ATOMIC ULTIMATUM

The atomic ultimatum, however, was not delivered. And after 1946, the illusory optimism of the LFA as to a swift turn in international events slowly evaporated. *Laisves Varpas* (Freedom Bell), a newspaper of the LFA, wrote in one of its issues in that year:

> Every day we suffer the brutalities of the bolshevik enemy by paying with the blood of our brethren and the cries of our

92

innocent people who are being murdered or deported. We wonder whether the world knows of our sufferings and our difficult and heroic struggle for the rights and the freedom of mankind, whose democratic ideals the leaders of the Western Democracies have proclaimed. Every drop of blood spilled in our fight against bolshevist tyranny is a sacrifice not only for Lithuania's freedom, but for that of the whole world.

In the months that followed, reality methodically and pitilessly destroyed whatever hopes remained. LFA emissaries, who returned to Lithuania from the free world in the summer of 1947, brought news that gave no reason to expect a change in the situation in Lithuania in the near future.

Another bitter disappointment was the failure of the Vatican to react to the "letter of the Roman Catholics of the Republic of Lithuania to His Holiness Pius XII," delivered by envoys of the Lithuanian underground in 1948. The only positive result of this message was an intensification of the Radio Vatican programs in Lithuanian. But the request that the Holy Father proclaim a Lithuanian Day to the Catholics of the world (as Pope Benedict XV had done in 1917), the appeal for a public statement of comfort and consolation to the Lithuanian Catholics by Pope Pius XII, and the request that the Vatican transmit the plea of the Lithuanian Catholics to the United Nations, evoked no response.

The letter of the Lithuanian Catholics to Pope Pius XII was at the same time an appeal to the conscience of the free world. More than that, the letter contained a warning that later proved of great significance:

Two hundred million multi-national people of the Soviet Union, including ourselves, are made to work night and day at manufacturing weapons to enslave the world. . . . Bolshevism is ready to destroy the world's culture and Christianity. Let us not deceive ourselves—Bolshevism is stronger than many of us think. The possession of atomic power is lulling the world to sleep. *Bolshevism will soon have weapons of the same potency.*

The letter was dated September 24, 1947. In 1949 the USSR exploded its first atom-bomb.

The warning was, of course, ignored by the free world. The LFA envoy who crossed the Iron Curtain to deliver the warning complained in his report to the LFA command, in 1949:

Our attempts to have broadcasts in the Lithuanian language initiated by various radio stations of the West are still blocked by obstacles. The BBC remains silent, despite appeals both through underground and diplomatic channels. The same attitude prevails in the Voice of America.* The situation is similar in Paris.

As the illusory optimism of the freedom fighters began to crumble amidst bitter reality, their former boundless faith in Western assistance changed to bitter disillusionment with the West:

They abandoned us to death in Yalta and Postdam. . . . They continue to repeat the same errors—they do not dare

---

* The Voice of America began broadcasts in the Lithuanian language on February 16, 1951. Exceptionally popular in Lithuania were the VOA broadcasts from Munich, initiated in 1952. Yet these broadcasts were cancelled in 1958.

to raise their voice in protest against the annihilation of our nation; they refuse to realize that we . . . are continuing the struggle. . . .

The majority of the LFA command, however, although it recognized that without Western assistance it was powerless to change the situation, did not succumb to pessimism. These LFA leaders reasoned that sooner or later the battle of the Lithuanian nation for freedom would find proper recognition in the free world. At the same time, the LFA command saw that its main task was now "to continue the fight for freedom by methods which would enable us to maintain our struggle until the necessary juncture."

This realization meant a change not only in tactics but also in the strategy of the LFA war against the USSR. It meant a revision of tasks and of the entire organization. It meant a step toward the "demobilization" of Lithuanian armed resistance.

IX

ENDURING RESISTANCE

. . . Keep your patience proud;
The bitter toil shall not be lost,
The rebel thought unbowed. . . .
————A. S. PUSHKIN

DEMOBILIZATION—NOT SURRENDER

The unfavorable evolution of international events for a speedy liberation of Lithuania was not the only reason for the LFA's decision to end armed resistance against the USSR.

The eight years of the war against Soviet forces had thinned the ranks of the freedom fighters. One detachment of the LFA, for instance, had lost seventy-two men and had fifty-nine wounded in the course of one year. As LFA forces were divided into nine districts, each with four or five detachments, the average yearly losses in dead and wounded can be set at almost 5,500. The entire war, 1944-1952, probably cost the LFA something more than 30,000 men. Most painful was the fact that the death toll took ninety per cent of the LFA cadres. The training of new cadres became impossible without the assistance of the free world.

Furthermore, the plentiful supplies of light arms and ammunition, which had fallen into LFA hands immediately after World War II, became exhausted. The annual losses of one LFA detachment, for instance, averaged out to 14 machine-guns and 76 other firearms. On this basis, the yearly losses of the LFA must have reached over 500 machine-guns and over 3000 other firearms, while the entire war must have consumed a total of 4000 machine-guns and 25,000 other weapons. The only remaining sources of replenishment of arms supplies were NKVD or Soviet Army munition depots. But raids on these depots became more and more costly and difficult.

After the Lithuanian farmers had been forcibly herded into kolkhozes, the situation of the LFA became even more grave. The collectivization pauperized the farmers to an unimaginable extent, and the provisioning of the freedom fighters with food and shelter grew more difficult with each passing day. The kolkhoz system also enabled the NKVD to expand its network of agents throughout the Lithuanian countryside.

Finally, the failure of the free world to support the LFA, either materially or morally, provided grist for the NKVD propaganda mills.

Under such conditions, it became impossible to maintain unified command over a functioning underground army, scattered as it was in small groups throughout all Lithuania. An LFA disengagement from armed hostilities against the USSR became inevitable.

LFA units were now faced with the task of "demobilizing" their men, i.e., returning them to the legal status of inhabitants of occupied Lithuania. And here the LFA agents and informers within the Soviet administration and the Communist party apparatus of Lithuania were extremely helpful.

To escape the suspicion of the NKVD, the "demobiliza-tion" of the LFA could not be conducted on a mass scale. It was carried out gradually, though at a more rapid pace after Stalin's death, and was deemed concluded in 1955.

Individual freedom fighters and small groups of between two and five persons continued armed resistance even after the "demobilization." Thus, on March 22, 1956, the State Security Committee appealed to "persons still in hiding" to take advantage of the Soviet amnesty. Clashes between NKVD troops and armed freedom fighters, who lost three men in one such encounter, have been reported in the press of occupied Lithuania as recently as 1959.

These sporadic forays by remnants of the LFA do not play a significant role in the new phase of the Lithuanian resist-ance against Soviet domination. At the same time, the "demo-bilized" freedom fighters, a few cases excepted, have not reconciled themselves to the present situation and have not capitulated to the Kremlin's current policy toward Lithu-ania. This is vividly exemplified by a continuing popular resistance through peaceful means.

RESISTANCE BY PEACEFUL MEANS

Passive resistance in Lithuania began with the Soviet occupation; it was overshadowed by the LFA's war against the USSR. But since the demobilization of the armed under-ground, this resistance by peaceful means is especially distinct in all spheres of Lithuanian life.

Economic resistance attained its peak intensity in the period of the forcible collectivization of Lithuanian farmers (1948-1950). Ninety-nine per cent of the Lithuanian farm-

98

ing population unanimously refused to accept voluntarily the revival of serfdom in the form of the kolkhoz system. When the kolkhoz system was imposed on Lithuanian farmers, they responded with a mass boycott. Not even the most drastic measures of the Kremlin—the mass deportations of the farmers in 1948, 1949, 1950—were able to break down that boycott, which continues even today. Although the kolkhozes and sovkhozes cover 95 per cent of Lithuania's agricultural land, they produce, according to Soviet data itself, only 39.2 per cent of the total meat production and 35 per cent of the total milk output. On the remaining five per cent of land that has been left for private cultivation, Lithuanian farmers manage to raise 60.8 per cent of the total meat and 65 per cent of the total milk output.

The tendency of Lithuanian passive resistance has been described by a number of Western newspapermen. One of these, Mr. Demaree Bess, wrote in the October 31, 1959, issue of the *Saturday Evening Post*:

> It is remarkable how tenaciously these peoples (Lithuanian, Latvian, Estonian) cling to their traditional languages and customs. That is especially notable in the rural communities, where the Balts have stubbornly resisted Moscow's efforts to impose Russian style collectivization upon them. I believe they have won a partial victory. . . . The Baltic countryside as seen from my airplane, with widely spaced individual farmhouses, more nearly resembled our New England than Russia. . . . Baltic farmers could not be herded into villages. So most Baltic so-called . . . collective farms are quite different from those in Russia. I talked to dozens of these farm people. . . . A number of them had returned recently after years in Russia. The way they talked showed that their spirit had not been broken. . . .

The Roman Catholic Church in Lithuania is one of the strongest bastions of Lithuanian resistance by peaceful means, and is therefore ceaselessly exposed to vicious attacks by the Kremlin and its Lithuanian puppets. The rulers of the Kremlin—in the eras both of Stalin and Khrushchev—have shown as much zeal in their program to destroy the Lithuanian Roman Catholic Church as in that designed to annihilate the LFA. Nevertheless, the Church in Lithuania has not only been able to withstand all these pressures, but has even strengthened its influence, and now encompasses not only the faithful, but all patriotic Lithuanians. The Church in Lithuania today is more than a community of Roman Catholics; it is the only Lithuanian national institution which has maintained its ideological and organizational independence from the Kremlin. As observed by Wanda Gawronska, a correspondent of the Italian magazine *Il Tiempo,* who visited Lithuania in 1960, "to attend church services here has the same value as to protest . . . which is the only means left for the Baltic people to show that they do not accept the present political situation."

The cultural resistance in Lithuania, like that of religion, has inherited the experiences gathered during Czarist Russian rule in Lithuania in the 19th century. Cultural resistance at that time continued for forty years, and ended with the victory of the Lithuanians.

Today Soviet Marxism seeks to replace the spiritual uniqueness and cultural originality of the captive nations with the gray uniformity of so-called Soviet culture. Within the sphere of Soviet control, the Communist party regulates every segment of cultural life. Artists are told what and how to create; they are bribed with financial rewards and threatened with enforced silence. The ultimate goal of Soviet cultural policy in captive Lithuania is the destruction of the very soul of the Lithuanian people. The Soviet administration endeavors to deprive the Lithuanians of their personal and national identity by:

(a) the eradication or destruction of Lithuanian national traditions and customs;

(b) falsification of Lithuanian history and removal of historic monuments;

(c) forcible imposition of Soviet atheism and the Soviet "versions" of dignity, truth, morality, freedom and democracy;

(d) imposition of Kremlin dogmas, as the sole and binding criteria for creative work, on Lithuanian writers, artists, scientists and other intellectuals;

(e) corruption of the Lithuanian language with Russianisms and the Communist jargon;

(f) glorification of all that is Soviet Russian and isolation of Lithuania from the cultural life of the free world;

(g) abolition of the freedoms of thought, conscience and expression.

Khrushchev's hope is that the growing disillusionment of the Lithuanians with the West, together with ceaseless Russification and communization, as well as the corrosive work of time, will turn Lithuanians into faceless, obedient slaves of the great Soviet ant-hill.

One of the greatest hopes for Lithuania's future lies in the fact that a new generation now stands in the forefront of resistance against the Soviet drive to distort the Lithuanian

101

national culture. Young Lithuanian writers, painters, composers and scholars refuse—in the words of Professor Ernest Simmons—"to kill within themselves the desire to convey a personal vision of humanity in their works." They not only refuse to bow to the precepts of the Communist "New Class," but they also openly defy them. In 1960, fifteen teachers were purged from the Vilnius University for "nationalist tendencies" and "ideological errors." An open revolt by young Lithuanian writers against the dogma of "socialist realism" in the fall of 1959 was reported in the weekly *Literatura ir Menas* last year. The stand of the young generation of intellectuals is best expressed in the slogan publicly circulated in Lithuania during and after the "thaw" in the empire: "Let us not retreat from the broad positions we have occupied; let us widen them!"

Thus, although LFA armed resistance in Lithuania lies in the past, the war on the Amber Coast goes on.

X

THE EXAMPLE OF LITHUANIAN RESISTANCE

*No man is an island, entire of itself;
every man is a piece of the continent,
a part of the main; if a clod be washed
away by the sea, Europe is the less, as
well as if a promontory were, as well as
if a manor of thy friends or of thine
own were; any man's death diminishes
me. . . .*

—JOHN DONNE

The history of the operations of the LFA, until now almost entirely unknown in the West, takes on a painful and perhaps especially useful relevance in the precarious world situation today. That history shows the willingness of the Soviets ruthlessly to commit massive resources—one might almost say, unlimited military power—to the attainment of their imperial and colonial ends. That history shows also what real successes can be effected by a relatively minute force, operating in the population of one of the small nations of the world, with wholly inadequate armament or other logistic support. The heroes who perished in the LFA possessed another category of weapon—that of a determination, a persistance and a courage which one is tempted to call absolute. These qualities, together with an ingenuity which

103

somehow contrived makeshifts amidst a ridiculous poverty of means, brought results that may tax the imagination of those in the West who now, at this late date, begin to sense the scope of the Soviet drive to power.

Current developments throughout the Indo-Chinese peninsula, as well as recent events in Cuba and Africa, have shown hideously the key importance of guerilla warfare —which is merely a determined struggle by scattered, outnumbered forces against overwhelming odds—in so-called "border" areas of the world, which are in grave jeopardy today. The exploits of the LFA hold lessons for "neutralists," and others in the West, who hope to turn their eyes from a menace which has by no means diminished in the last decade, or who, still more irresponsibly, do not really care. As the periphery of the free world is eroded by incessant Soviet and Communist Chinese manoeuvres, it would be well to remember that the West does not possess an endless supply of small nations, the sacrifice of which, some may still unrealistically hope, will indefinitely postpone a confrontation between the free world and a dehumanized totalitarianism which, in its gratuitous and senseless power mania, can be called insane.

The fallen fighters of the LFA are still remembered and revered in the villages of Lithuania, where they died. They can perhaps now continue to serve the cause of freedom, if the free world will recognize their sacrifice, and find in it occasion and means to undertake comparable efforts. Lithuania is a nation which many westerners could not readily locate on the map. Yet it is close to all, too close, in a sense that should bring no comfortable reassurance. Tragically, many forget that the experience of the LFA can be repeated in any other country in the world, and that—in the worst event—a "West" might eventually no longer exist as a haven for those who still remain wishfully deluded or in different. In such a disaster, the exploits of the LFA will in fact become history, as it comprises events of an irrevocable past; but that history will then lie in silence, recorded no where.

CHRONOLOGY

1251: Establishment of the Lithuanian Kingdom.

1410: United Lithuanian-Polish armies defeat the Teutonic Order at Tannenberg.

1569: Lithuanian-Polish Commonwealth.

1795-1915: Lithuania under Russian rule.

1915-1918: Lithuania under German military occupation.

1918: Restoration of Lithuania's Independence (February 16).

1920: Peace Treaty with Soviet Russia (July 12).

1926: Non-Aggression Pact with the USSR (September 28).

1939: Secret Soviet-Nazi agreements concerning Lithuania (August 23, September 28).

1940: Soviet invasion of Lithuania (June 15).

1940: Mass arrests of Lithuanians by the NKVD (July 11).

1940: Mock elections to the "People's Diet" (July 14).

1940: USA reaction against Soviet aggression (July 23).

1940: Forcible incorporation of Lithuania into the USSR (August 3).

1940: Beginning of organized Lithuanian resistance (in October).

1941: First mass deportations (June 13-20).

1941: Armed revolt against Soviet occupation (June 23).

1941: Suppression of the Provisional Lithuanian Government by the Nazis (August 5).

1941: Atlantic Charter signed (August 14).

1944: Re-occupation of Lithuania by Soviet armies.

1944: Beginning of guerilla warfare against the Soviets.

1953: Investigation of Soviet aggression against the Baltic States by the Select House Committee (July 27).

BIBLIOGRAPHY

Anima, Bern, Switzerland, Vol. I, 1950.

Baltiska Nyheter, Stockholm, September 26, 1944.

Baltic Review, Stockholm, Vol. II, No. 2.

Current News on the Lithuanian Situation, Lithuanian Legation, Washington, D.C., Vol. I, Nos. 1-24; Vol. II, Nos. 2, 4-8, 10-12; Vol. III, Nos. 1-8, 11-13, 15, 18; Vol. IV, Nos. 2, 4-12; Vol. V, Nos. 3-4, 71-72, 73, 75-77; Vol. VI, Nos. 7-8, 11-16; Vol. IX, No. 1.

Daily Mail, London, January 5, 1947 (Continental Edition).

Genocide: Lithuania's Threefold Tragedy, by K. Pelekis, Germany, 1949.

Hinter dem Eisernen Vorhang, Germany, 1948.

I Laisve (Toward Freedom), Lithuanian Quarterly, New York-Chicago, Nos. 40, 42-49, 51, 52, 56, 59-62.

In the Name of the Lithuanian People, Germany, 1945.

Jaunimo Gretos (Ranks of Youth), monthly, Vilnius, No. 4 of 1954; No. 8 of 1957; Nos. 3, 9-11 of 1958; No. 9 of 1960.

Komjaunimo Tiesa (The Komsomol Truth), daily, Vilnius, No. 236 of 1960; Nos. 14, 68, 128 of 1961.

Lietuviu Enciklopedija (Lithuanian Encyclopedia), Vol. XXII, 1960.

Lietuvos Pionierius (Lithuanian Pioneer), semiweekly, Vilnius, Nos. 40, 99 of 1958; Nos. 3, 9, 67, 69 of 1958; Nos. 9, 13, 38, 39, 47, 54 of 1960.

Lithuania Under the Sickle and Hammer, by J. Petruitis, Cleveland, Ohio, 1945.

Lithuanian Bulletin, Lithuanian American Information Center, New York, Vol. V, Nos. 7-8, 9-10; Vol. VI, Nos. 1-10; Vol. VII, Nos. 1-3, 7-12; Vol. VIII, Nos. 7-12; Vol. IX, Nos. 1-12.

Lithuania's Fight for Freedom, by E. J. Harrison, New York, 1952.

Lituanus, Lithuanian Quarterly (in English), New York, Nos. 3-4 of 1955, Nos. 2-3 of 1956, No. 3 of 1957, Nos. 2-3 of 1960.

Nepaskelbtas Karas Lietuvoje (Undeclared War in Lithuania), Report from Lithuania by Supreme Committee for the Liberation of Lithuania, 1946.

Newsletter on Contemporary Communism, New York, May 1, 1946.

Partizanai uz Gelezinês Uzdangos (Partisans Behind the Iron Curtain), by J. Daumantas, Chicago, 1950. A factual history of the LFA written by one of its leaders who were able to reach the West.

Reports of the Select House Committee on Soviet Aggression, Washington, D.C., 1954.

Santarve (Alliance), Lithuanian Quarterly, London, No. 4 of 1953; Nos. 1, 2, 4, 5, 7-10 of 1954; Nos. 2, 4, 5 of 1955.

Svyturys (Beacon), biweekly, Vilnius, No. 9 of 1957; Nos. 2, 4, 19 of 1958; Nos. 6, 24 of 1960; Nos. 14, 15 of 1961.

Tarybinis Mokytojas (Soviet Teacher), semiweekly, Vilnius, Nos. 73, 78 of 1961.

Tiesa (Truth), daily, Vilnius, No. 299 of 1957; Nos. 34, 57, 70, 71, 215, 272, 280, 289 of 1958; Nos. 133-135, 139-154, 156-179, 301-303 of 1959; No. 42 of 1960.

Valstieciu Laikrastis (Peasants' Newspaper), semiweekly, Vilnius, Nos. 50, 51, 52 of 1960.